THEY'LL HAVE TO FOLLOW YOU!

To Howard —
Please enjoy the book —

11/14/09

THEY'LL HAVE TO FOLLOW YOU!

THE TRIUMPH OF THE
GREAT WHITE FLEET

MARK ALBERTSON

TATE PUBLISHING *& Enterprises*

Published by Tate Publishing & Enterprises, LLC
127 E. Trade Center Terrace | Mustang, Oklahoma 73064 USA
1.888.361.9473 | www.tatepublishing.com

Tate Publishing is committed to excellence in the publishing industry. The company reflects the philosophy established by the founders, based on Psalms 68:11,
"The Lord gave the word and great was the company of those who published it."

Book design copyright © 2007 by Tate Publishing, LLC. All rights reserved.
Cover design by Leah LeFlore
Cover photo courtesy Naval Historical Center NH001836.
Interior design by Steven Jeffrey

Published in the United States of America

ISBN: 978-1-60462-145-7
1. History: Military: Naval   2. United States: Twentieth Century (1900-1945)
07.10.26

DEDICATION

To my family. May they understand and forgive the loss
in quality time forfeited in deference to the preservation
of American History.

TABLE OF CONTENTS

ACKNOWLEDGMENTS

They'll Have to Follow You! is the companion volume to the previously released *USS Connecticut: Constitution State Battleship*. The latter is the story of the flagship of the Great White Fleet, while the former relates the adventures of the entire task force.

When I began the quest to record the history of battleship *Connecticut*, the saga of the round-the-world cruise proved so compelling that it seemed a natural progression to follow through with a work on the entire fleet. It is my earnest hope that the reader will find both volumes welcome editions to the history of early twentieth century America.

I want to thank my editor, Kylie Lyons and the rest of the gang at Tate Publishing for their efforts in this endeavor. I also want to thank my wife, Rose Marie, whose skills on the computer came through on more than one occasion. But most of all I am deeply indebted to the twenty-sixth president of the United States, Theodore Roosevelt, and the 14,500 officers and men of the Great White Fleet, for without them, there would be no story to tell.

The Author

INTRODUCTION

On March 9, 1862, two of the most extraordinary combatants in the history of naval warfare clashed at sea. To some they were known as the "Colossus of Roads" and the "Cheesebox on a Raft." To history they were known as the *Virginia* and the *Monitor*. Their four-hour slugfest proved largely indecisive. Yet they forever altered the way navies fought at sea. They also formed the embryo in the evolution of the American battleship.

The *Virginia*, known originally as the *Merrimac*, had been a steam frigate of 350 tons and forty guns. She had been burned and left derelict by Union forces upon evacuation of the Gosport Navy Yard. Rebuilt and refloated by the Confederates, the warship took on a whole new look. She was given a superstructure that rose seven feet above the deck and stretched 178 feet amidships. Protection amounted to twenty inches of pine beneath four inches of oak. Four inches of railroad iron overlaid the timber. The sides were sloped thirty-five degrees to allow for maximum shell deflection. Armament consisted of two six-inch and two seven-inch rifles and six nine-inch smoothbore guns. A 1,500-pound ram protruded ominously from the bow. Length overall was 263 feet. Total complement was three hundred hands, most of whom were Confederate soldiers.

The Union challenger was much smaller in size and simpler in design. *Monitor* looked very much like a World

War II submarine. She had a low-slung hull, which was tapered fore and aft. She was 142 feet from stem to stern and had a beam of forty-one feet five inches. Protection amounted to a one-inch deck and five inches of side armor.

Topside there was not much in the way of a superstructure—just a pair of collapsible funnels, a small armored conning tower, and the ironclad's raison d'etre, a turret. The last named was the brainchild of a New York-based Swedish inventor named John Ericsson. His revolving gun platform stood nine feet by twenty feet across. Eight inches of armor shielded the crew who manned two eleven-inch smoothbore guns, each of which threw a 166-pound steel ball.

The sea-keeping characteristics of both vessels were abysmal. In fact, *Monitor* was nearly swamped while being towed from New York to Hampton Roads. These ironclads were bred for combat in such areas as coastal waters, rivers, and inlets. In terms of maneuverability, *Monitor* was quite the hoofer in comparison to *Virginia*, which was a plodder. The Confederate's top speed was barely five knots. And its turning radius was so poor that it took thirty minutes to bring *Virginia* round 180 degrees. Yet despite being more nimble, *Monitor* boasted a turret. This enabled the gun crew to fire on any point on the compass without changing the ship's direction. This was the most revolutionary aspect of *Monitor's* design. In the future, ships would no longer have to change course to train their guns, merely traverse a turret.

On March 8, the Confederate States Navy gained the tactical advantage when the *Virginia* sank the Union warships *Cumberland* and *Congress*. *Monitor* arrived on the scene the next day. The ensuing clash of the ironclads ended in a stalemate, a stalemate that cost the South its earlier advantage. The result was that the Union blockade was saved and the North retained command of the seas. Any hopes the Confederacy had of foreign intervention on its behalf were dashed. This was a strategic turning point in the American Civil War, a turning point every bit as significant as Meade's defeat of Lee at Gettysburg.

The majority of Americans had little interest in the advances of military technology after five years of blood-letting. The focus turned instead to domestic concerns as the nation attempted to rebuild. The period known as Reconstruction was also a period of isolation. Yet over the next forty-five years, events both national and international conspired to change the course of American history as well as the nation's standing in the world. And nowhere can this be seen more clearly than in America's understanding of the importance of sea power.

The evolution that began on March 9, 1862, came to fruition nearly forty-seven years later on February 22, 1909, George Washington's birthday. What began at Hampton Roads had come full circle to end at Hampton Roads, as President Theodore Roosevelt's Atlantic Fleet Battleship Force returned from its epic round-the-world cruise. The sixteen battleships that had sailed over forty-six thousand miles were the products of a young and vibrant nation employing the advantages of the Industrial Revolution to its fullest. It was the culmination of success by a navy that had first attempted to control the seas with ironclads that were barely seaworthy, to a fleet of first-class battleships that had circumnavigated the globe.

Forever known to history as the Great White Fleet,

Theodore Roosevelt's battleships captured the imagination of the world. The cruise proved an immense public relations success for the Navy. Relations were fostered with nations that hitherto had been little more than names on a map; while relations with familiar capitals were enhanced. The cruise highlighted such deficiencies in American battleship design as the placement of armor and ammunition hoists. The lack of American logistic support was also laid bare, ramming home the lesson that without an adequate homegrown merchant marine, control of the seas was all but impossible.

Yet in the end, Theodore Roosevelt's gambit proved to be an enterprise of immense historical significance. It demonstrated America's ability to transfer power from the Atlantic Ocean to the Pacific. Valuable lessons learned in the projection of sea power would later pay handsome dividends in two global conflicts. But of greater importance is that Roosevelt's gambit elevated the United States to the ranks of the global powers. In so doing it proved not only a turning point in American history, but in the history of the world. Such was the triumph of the Great White Fleet.

ISOLATION TO GLOBALIZATION

April 9, 1865, is one of the most significant dates in American history. It is the day General Robert E. Lee surrendered his tattered Army of Northern Virginia to the victorious Union Forces of General Ulysses S. Grant. So ended the bloodiest war in American history. But the significance of the date goes beyond the simple termination of an internecine struggle that had pitted brother against brother. It is also the date that the United States of America decided to shut out the rest of the world.

The Civil War had nearly torn the nation asunder. Time was needed to bring the country together. Time to heal old wounds. Time to rebuild the shattered South. Westward expansion resumed, with millions seeking their fortunes on the virgin lands west of the Mississippi River. Continental expansion reduced the focus of the military to its land campaigns against the Indian nations of the west. The strategic significance of sea power foundered on the rocks of national seclusion. However, nothing could stem the tide of international trade, and the desire for self-imposed quarantine failed in the end to withstand the inexorable encroachment of global commerce.

At the beginning of the nineteenth century, global commerce totaled some $1.5 billion. By 1850, it was $4 billion. By 1900, it was a whopping $24 billion. The Industrial Revolution had reached critical mass and the resulting cataclysm of economic activity was shrinking the globe. Britain, following the Napoleonic Wars, emerged much like the United States would later on, following the collapse of the Soviet Union, as the one true global power. By 1900, with her vast colonial empire, Rule Britannia accounted for one-quarter of the world's trade.

For the United States, international trade was eating away at seclusion. This can be seen in the decline of its merchant marine. In 1860, the merchant fleet of the United States was 2,500,000 tons, second to that of Great Britain. But due to losses incurred during the Civil War and attention paid to such isolationist pursuits as westward expansion, the American merchant marine was allowed to languish. The United States could not keep up with Great Britain, where government subsidies and the conversion from planking to steel allowed Britain to build ships in greater numbers and build them cheaply. Prior to the American Civil War, seventy-two percent of American goods were carried by American bottoms. By 1913, this was down to a paltry nine percent.

However, America's growing economic power and booming westward expansion soon gave rise to the fear of foreign incursions by the imperialist powers from Europe, in particular, Great Britain. But naval strategy as viewed by Washington had not progressed much beyond the idea of shielding the East Coast with fortified strong points and coast defense ships reminiscent of Civil War types. Such a strategy fell woefully short of appreciating the strategic significance of sea power. And in 1873, there occurred an incident on the high seas that laid bare American weakness.

The affair was the *Virginius* Incident. The *Virginius* was a Scottish-built steamer that had served the Confederacy during the Civil War. She was a side wheeler of two hundred feet and 491 tons. Beginning in 1870, the steamer had been used to run guns and supplies to the insurrectionists in Cuba. In late October 1873, *Virginius* left Kingston for Haiti. In command was Joseph Fry, a veteran of the Confederate States Navy. In Haiti, *Virginius* took on a load of three hundred rifles, ammunition, gunpowder, and other stores for the rebels. Off Guantanamo Bay, *Virginius* was intercepted by the Spanish corvette *Tornado*. The gun runner, flying the American flag, was interned with its crew in Santiago.

Among the passengers and crew were Americans, Britons, and Cubans. Fifty-three were executed as pirates. Among those killed was Captain Fry. The rest were spared when the British man-of-war, HMS *Niobe,* appeared off Santiago. Its captain demanded an end to the executions or he threatened that he would reduce the city to rubble.

Two years later, Madrid settled a claim of reparations with Washington for $80,000. Years later the incident would serve as a rallying cry for Americans during the Spanish-American War. However, no amount of money could hide the inept American response: It took the Royal Navy to save American lives. The result was the authorization by Congress for a few cruisers and coast defense monitors. This was hardly the response indicative of an appreciation of the dismal state of the United States Navy. It would be another ten years before a clear understanding of America's plight sank in. This resulted in the cruisers *Atlanta, Boston,* and *Chicago* and the dispatch ship *Dolphin.* These were followed by two armored cruisers, the ill-fated *Maine* and *Texas.* These units formed the core of the "New Navy."

Then, in 1890, Captain Alfred Thayer Mahan, USN, published a work that was to have a worldwide impact: *The Influence of Sea Power Upon History, 1660–1783.* Here Mahan outlined the reality that without sea power, the ability to project power globally and command the seas was all but impossible. A strong and viable fleet was necessary to keep enemy forces distant. Since the defeat of the Spanish Armada in 1588, Britain's Royal Navy had enjoyed undisputed supremacy at sea. Mahan's treatise changed all that. Germany, Italy, France, Russia, and the United States commenced major programs of warship construction; in particular, battleships.

For the United States, the threat of an Anglo incursion into North America receded with the advent of German power. It was the closing chapter of the Age of Imperialism. Germany and Italy, newly arrived on the world scene as sovereign nations, sought their rightful places under the sun by attempting to grab colonies overseas. Such agendas of aggrandizement were possible only with sea power. This was particularly true with regards to Germany. In 1898, the *Flottengesetz,* or Naval Law was passed in Germany and set the Kaiser's navy on an ambitious program of warship construction. This development did not go unnoticed in Washington.

German intentions had been viewed with suspicion years before with Teutonic intrigues in Samoa. In 1878, Samoa had been colonized by American, British, and German traders. Ten years later, a tripartite protectorate had been established over the islands. Trouble ensued when in 1899, the king of Samoa died. The result was a violent tug-of-war over the succession to the throne. During a bombardment by British and American warships, the German consulate was struck by several shells. The United States issued an apology, which the German Government duly accepted. But then Berlin turned around and suggested to London an alliance to evict the Americans from the islands. Britain balked and the "Samoan Crisis" became front page news.

The issue was settled on November 8, 1899. Germany acquired Western Samoa. The United States retained its holdings, including its naval station at Pago Pago. The British relinquished their holdings and grabbed Tonga and the Solomon Islands. The Samoan Crisis was not the only incident in the Pacific involving Germany. In 1897, Berlin used the excuse of the murder of two missionaries to order the occupation of Kiao-Chow. The Chinese port had been coveted as a coaling station. Other European powers began to occupy other Chinese coastal cities as well. Then, in 1898, while Spain was embroiled with the United States, Berlin persuaded Madrid to sell the island chains of the Palaus, Carolines, and Marianas. German belligerence carried forth to the Philippines as well. Admiral Dewey had just defeated the Spanish fleet when German Admiral von Diedrichs appeared with five warships. Undaunted, Admiral Dewey suggested that the German admiral make his way out the same way he came in or fight it out. Newly arrived British and Japanese squadrons kept the antagonists apart, and the American occupation of the Philippines was allowed to proceed.

Victory in the Spanish-American War raised the United States to the ranks of the imperialist powers. This was a development that seemed all but inevitable. Thomas

Jefferson had set the pace in 1803 with the Louisiana Purchase. By the end of the nineteenth century, American expansion to the West Coast had reached its zenith. Yet as a young and vibrant nation with an unquenchable desire for new markets and inventions, the urge to overflow its borders was all but impossible to suppress.

Defeat of Spain had other implications as well. In exercise of the Monroe Doctrine, Spain, a European colonial power, had been evicted from the Western Hemisphere. Puerto Rico became an American possession. And Cuba became an independent nation. In the Pacific, the defeat of Spain saw the advent of American hegemony in the Philippines. Guam in the Marianas became an American possession. And the United States annexed the Sandwich Islands (Hawaii).

American inroads in the Pacific opened competition with that up-and-coming power in the Far East, Japan. Not long after the arrival of Commodore Perry in 1853, Japan quickly grasped the realities of the world. Many of her neighbors had incurred the encroachments of western colonists—India, China, and Southeast Asia. It was decided early on that this was not going to happen to Japan. She industrialized, becoming the most powerful nation in Asia. She also embarked on an armaments program, focusing on naval arms. And in 1894, Japan decided to join the ranks of the imperialists by going to war with China.

Against the outmoded Chinese fleet, the Imperial Navy quickly decided the issue and won control of the Yellow Sea. On land, the German-trained Japanese Army swept the Chinese out of the Korean Peninsula in less than eight weeks. Next, Imperial troops stormed Manchuria, took the Liaotung Peninsula and Port Arthur, and threatened to move south on Peking. China sued for peace.

On April 17, 1895, the Treaty of Shimonoseki ended Chinese occupation of Korea and turned over to Japan the island of Formosa (Taiwan), the Pescadores Islands, and the Liaotung Peninsula. Japan earned "most favored nation" status in China and forced Peking to pay a large indemnity.

The speed of the Japanese conquests stunned European observers. Three of them, France, Russia, and Germany, took exception to Japanese encroachments and threatened action if Port Arthur and the Liaotung Peninsula were not returned to China. Japan was forced to acquiesce in the face of such opposition. At home, the humiliation caused a backlash in Japanese public opinion. In response, Japan doubled its armaments budget. Beginning in 1897, Japan added four battleships, sixteen cruisers, and twenty-three destroyers to its fleet over the next six years. In 1902, Great Britain and Japan forged an alliance in response to Czarist ambitions in Asia. Russian designs in Manchuria threatened British positions in China. In turn, the Japanese saw the Russians as a threat to their interests in Korea. The alliance obligated either party to come to other's aid in case of war with Russia, but only if Russia attacked with an ally, for example, France. Politically for Tokyo, Britain recognized Japanese interests in Korea and China. For London, it permitted the redeployment of naval units to home waters in response to the growing German threat.

In 1903, Tokyo engaged the Czarist government in negotiations designed to solve the Manchurian question. The talks proved fruitless. Russia refused to withdraw troops from Manchuria and even sent troops into Korea in the beginning of February 1904. On February 8, Japan launched a surprise attack on the Russian Far East Fleet at Port Arthur. The next day, Tokyo declared war.

Japanese troops poured into Korea. They swept up the peninsula, pushed into Manchuria, and laid siege to Port Arthur. The latter was finally taken in January 1905. Meanwhile, the Russian Baltic Fleet, under Admiral Zinovy Rodzhestvensky, was on its way to save Russian honor. This poor excuse for a fleet sailed over eighteen thousand miles to no purpose, save for destruction. On May 25, 1905, Admiral Heihachiro Togo's smaller but more efficient fleet met and utterly destroyed the enemy in Tsushima Strait.

President Theodore Roosevelt brokered the peace treaty in Portsmouth, New Hampshire, on September 5, 1905. Japanese interests in Manchuria and Korea were recognized. Within two months, Korea was deemed a Japanese protectorate, and in five years it was annexed. The Japanese were still disappointed that they received no indemnity and were given no other territorial concessions. However, Japan's victory shocked the world, for an Asian power had defeated an important European power.

The defeat of Russian naval power proved a significant development. The 1902 Anglo-Japanese Alliance had been brokered to thwart Russian Asiatic designs. With the crushing defeat of the Czar's navy, Russian power had been broken. Yet Britain still faced the growing threat of German naval might. Relief was forthcoming from two fronts: The period of 1902–04 saw a decline in French naval power. This permitted the Royal Navy to recall units from the Mediterranean to bolster the Home Fleet. Then, in 1905, Britain and Japan renewed their 1902 alliance.

The renewal was for ten years and required the military cooperation of the signatories if either was attacked by another single power. This enabled London to recall five battleships from the Pacific. The dilemma for Britain was that preservation of its Far East possessions might now entail assistance from the ambitious Japanese. At the same time, there was a growing realization in London that, on the other side of the globe, converging strategic interests portended cooperation with the dynamic United States. Yet there was no denying the new reality in Asia: British retrenchment had left Japan with the most powerful navy in the Pacific.

The change in global dynamics did not escape the attention of policymakers in Washington. The period between 1898 to 1907 was one of growing American interest in the Pacific Basin. The Philippines had been taken from Spain. Guam was made an American possession and Hawaii was annexed. American business recognized the advantage of opening Asian markets. The need to protect such interests necessitated the appropriate naval response. So the United States embarked on an ambitious battleship construction program.

By 1900, six battleships were in service, three in the Atlantic and three in the Pacific. Then came the assassination of President William McKinley. Theodore Roosevelt assumed the presidency. The former Rough Rider was a confirmed navalist and committed to the United States becoming a first-rate naval power. Over the next seven years, fifteen battleships joined the fleet. In just three decades, the United States Navy, which had been a token force of less importance than the Peruvian Navy, had risen to become the second most powerful navy in the world after the Royal Navy.

By 1906, the strategic outlook for American planners had changed. Concerns about German colonial designs on the Caribbean and South America seemed to abate. Though the High Seas Fleet was a force to be reckoned with, Germany was at an immense disadvantage on two counts: Most of the Kaiser's heavy ships lacked the cruising radius to be a long-range threat. And the larger Royal Navy was strategically placed to prevent a German breakout from the North Sea into the North Atlantic in time of war.

Concern then shifted to the Pacific region. Korea had been reduced to the status of a Japanese vassal. Tokyo continued to pursue its agenda in Manchuria, which many Americans viewed as a threat to the Open Door Policy of trade with China. Then there was the issue of Japanese emigration to the U.S. West Coast. Cheap Oriental labor was looked upon as a threat by those competing in the area's job market. This issue rankled Californians in particular. In many cities on the West Coast, such as San Francisco, angry protests grew into riots. The fires of discontent were fanned by those drumbeaters in the press who routinely espoused the "Yellow peril." The situation deteriorated to the extent that by 1906–07, a full-blown war scare had developed. With the resulting "Gentleman's Agreement" between Japan and the United States, Tokyo agreed to limit the number of workers emigrating to Hawaii and the West Coast. Many Americans doubted Japanese sincerity and failed to put much stock in anything that smacked of a mere handshake.

It was not until November 1908 that a potential Japanese-American conflict was averted with the Root-Takahira Agreement. The result was the recognition of the Open Door Policy and Chinese territorial integrity and independence. There would be mutual discussions between Washington and Tokyo in the event of future Pacific crises. American concerns about Japanese designs on the Philippines were, for the moment, ameliorated, while Washington acknowledged the reality of Japanese suzerainty over Korea and Japanese interests in Manchuria. In reality, it was an acceptance of Tokyo's version of the Monroe Doctrine, which would later become the Japanese militarists' agenda known as the Greater East Asia Co-Prosperity Sphere.

In 1907, diplomats from round the world gathered at The Hague in an attempt to curb the unrestrained growth in naval arms. HMS *Dreadnought* had been launched the year before and had changed the complexion of the naval arms race overnight. *Dreadnought* relegated every other battleship in the world obsolete. This spawned a new arms race, which resulted in battleships of greater size, speed, and firepower. Upwards of seventy vessels were ordered over the next three years, as nations sought to address fleet imbalances with neighbors or pursue regional or global agendas of strategic significance. Against the backdrop of disarmament talks, the strategic game of one-upmanship continued unabated and eventually won the day. The attempt at The Hague to limit the spread of more and deadly battleships was stillborn in the womb. That failure was realized nine years later when the Royal Navy and the High Seas Fleet squared off at Jutland.

The United States employed the Great White Fleet for the same reason that Britain and Germany did when they sent their fleets into action in the North Sea; that is, to demonstrate the ability to take control of the seas with an overwhelming display of naval might. However, unlike the celebrated clash off the Skagerrak, the round-the-world cruise accomplished its objective without a shot being fired in anger. This peaceful demonstration of naval power is the enduring legacy of the Great White Fleet and to the man most responsible for the cruise, Theodore Roosevelt. Like Thomas Jefferson, who set the pace of westward expansion with the Louisiana Purchase in 1803, Theodore Roosevelt set the United States on the path to becoming a global power with the sailing of the Great White Fleet, a journey that saw the United States eventually become the most powerful nation on the globe and made the twentieth century the American century.

PREPARATIONS

On July 27, 1907, the president gathered with his advisors at the Roosevelt home at Sagamore Hill in Oyster Bay, Long Island. Among the items on the table for discussion was the worsening situation in the Pacific. Despite the inflammatory bombast in certain areas of the American press and the uneasiness of the American people on the West Coast, President Roosevelt felt certain that war with Japan could be avoided. All the same, he ordered the navy to take certain precautions short of war. In the Philippines, coal was stockpiled for the Asiatic Fleet. Coastal defense guns earmarked for Cavite were rerouted to Subic Bay. The gunboats and monitors of the Asiatic Fleet were ordered to be concentrated at Subic, while the fleet's four armored cruisers were ordered home to the West Coast. The president also decided to send the Atlantic Fleet Battleship Force to the Pacific.

Such deployments could hardly escape the detection of the suspicious Japanese. Yet there was nothing latent or secret about the president's intent. His aim was clear: To show the Japanese that the United States was committed to its interests in the region and to do this through a course of actions that were meant to be construed as firm without being provocative. The shifting round of a few gunboats and cruisers was one thing. But how could the massive redeployment of battleships be construed as anything else but provocative?

Allegations appearing in the American press concerning U.S. battleships heading for the Pacific were denied by the White House. Yet concerns about raising tensions with Tokyo proved unfounded when Viscount Aoki, Japanese ambassador to the United States, assured the White House that the appearance of American warships in the Pacific would not be looked upon as a hostile act. This was followed quickly by pronouncements from the White House that plans for sending warships to the Pacific were in their "early stages." Then, in August, President Roosevelt announced that sixteen battleships of the Atlantic Fleet would sail round the South American continent on their way to San Francisco. Their route of return would be decided later.

Even the most novice of map readers could have made a pretty fair guess as to the fleet's route of return: Across the Pacific and Indian Oceans to the Suez Canal, and then across the Mediterranean to the Atlantic, or round the Cape of Good Hope and up the South Atlantic. And it would most likely be the former instead of the latter. For apart from saving time and coal, the former offered more of the port facilities needed to service the fleet. Plus, in transiting the Suez Canal, the president could impress the major European powers with the new long reach of his navy and do so in their own backyard.

The State Department was shut out of the early planning stages of the cruise. The show was the production of the White House and the Navy Department. The navy was eager to find out just how long it would take to move the fleet from Hampton Roads to San Francisco in time of war. This was the overriding military concern for the first leg of the voyage. At the same time, it was believed that fleet visits to strategically located ports in South America would demonstrate to these nations the commitment of the United States to the Monroe Doctrine.

By sending the fleet to the West Coast, the White House hoped to show the constituents there of the president's genuine concern for their defense. Such a demonstration would not only benefit the administration, but the Navy Department as well. For it was hoped that by showing the flag from coast to coast that it would raise in the American people an awareness of the importance of sea power and to instill in them a sense of pride in their navy. Such a public relations success would create a favorable atmosphere in Congress by which the navy would benefit with regards to budgetary considerations and procurement.

Building a fleet of warships is not possible without money. At the beginning of the twentieth century, the big ticket item in naval construction was the battleship. The battleship was the strategic weapon of its day. Without them, global foreign policy objectives were unattainable. Theodore Roosevelt thoroughly understood this concept. He had planned a show of force in the Pacific years before but was unable to do so because of the lack of capital ships. However, many of the battleships that had been laid down during the first years of his administration were available by July 1907. By then, ten new battleships had joined the fleet, with three more nearly ready to slide down the building ways.

But command of the seas required more than just big guns and armor plate. A sound system of support was as much a prerequisite as having combat ships in the exercise of sea power. That support system featured auxiliary vessels such as colliers, which kept the fleet supplied with coal, and port and repair facilities to keep the men-of-war in fighting trim. The classic example of an inadequate support structure was that of the Russian Baltic Fleet. It sailed eighteen thousand miles and, minus the proper auxiliaries and port facilities en route, arrived in no shape to fight a major engagement. On the other hand, the Imperial Japanese Navy was close to home and enjoyed a ready access to fuel supplies and docking facilities. When it came time for battle, the emperor's fleet was ready and eager to come to grips with the enemy and won a great victory.

The plight of the Russian Baltic Fleet haunted the Navy Department. It would be sending the Atlantic Fleet Battleship Force thousands of miles into the Pacific to impress a modern battle-tested navy that did not know defeat. An adversary who was close to his fuel supplies and docking facilities, while the untested American battle fleet could put into the Philippines to coal, the docking facilities there were far from those needed to keep a fleet in top fighting condition. This made the port and docking facilities on the West Coast that much more important.

It was expected that after rounding the South American continent, the Great White Fleet would need the port and docking facilities on the West Coast. Every ship in the fleet was to be put into dry dock, then overhauled and refurbished as if being made ready for combat in the Pacific. Question was just how good were the available port and docking facilities?

The outlook was pretty grim. The only navy yard on the entire West Coast that could accommodate battle-ships was the Puget Sound Navy Yard in Bremerton,

Washington. The Mare Island Navy Yard near San Francisco had a channel that was too shallow. Despite this oversight, work commenced in 1900 for a new dry dock to accommodate the fleet's battleships. Completion was set for 1907. However, the foundation was found to be too weak. So Mare Island was rendered useless to Roosevelt's fleet.

The only other dockyard available was Hunter's Point, also in San Francisco. Hunter's Point was a civilian dockyard and was owned by the San Francisco Dry Dock Company. It had been closed and slated for demolition due to the lack of utilization. President Roosevelt ordered the facility reopened and repaired. This was done and Hunter's Point was ready when the fleet came to call.

The lack of port and docking facilities on the West Coast served to underscore America's weakness as a Pacific naval power. This meant that any concentration of naval might in the Pacific could be only for the short term. Most of the major port and docking facilities were on the East Coast. Appreciation of the strategic significance of the Pacific Basin would come in time. But in 1907, Congress, for the most part, thought Atlantic Ocean. And congressional appropriations were based on this thinking. This is easy to understand since Washington D.C. was the seat of power and most of the influential constituencies were east of the Mississippi River.

A similar situation existed with regards to fuel. Coal was the fuel of the day. Coal was an extremely dirty fuel to handle, and its sooty, black plume could be seen from miles away. But coal was cheap and it was plentiful. Fleets obtained coal from two sources: land-based coaling stations and colliers. For an imperialist power like Great

Britain, its vast empire provided a worldwide network of coaling stations. Britain also had the world's largest merchant marine. With more than an ample supply of colliers, coal could be supplied to His Majesty's ships at any coaling station or mid-ocean rendezvous point. The United States enjoyed no such luxury.

When the Atlantic Fleet Battleship Force cruised the Atlantic or Caribbean, coaling was not an issue. The fleet was close to home, which meant its fuel supplies were close at hand. But to send sixteen battleships to the far-flung ends of the globe was something different. Here coaling would be more than just an issue, it would be the Achille's heel. The plight of Admiral Dewey's fleet before its historic engagement at Manila Bay offers a case in point. In Hong Kong and short of fuel, Dewey had to purchase a collier-load of coal from the British to replenish his bunkers. Yet Dewey's predicament paled in comparison to that of the aforementioned Russian Baltic Fleet.

Admiral Rodzhestvensky's fleet of forty-two warships left the Baltic Sea to engage an enemy half a world away. For him coal was the overriding concern. Czarist Russia was a landlocked empire. It virtually had no possessions along the entire route of sail. It was certain as sunrise that Britain would honor its commitment to Japan and supply not a crumb of coal. France, though on friendly terms with Russia, found it more expedient not to offend Britain by assisting the czar's navy. And to make matters worse for Admiral Rodzhestvensky, he was on a war cruise. And according to international law, most neutral ports would be closed to his ships.

An agreement was struck with the Hamburg-American Line in Germany. The half million tons of coal necessary to fuel Rodzhestvensky's fleet would be provided along the route by sixty German colliers. Coaling is a tough and dirty business in a port with adequate facilities. But at sea it is a thoroughly backbreaking job, especially if the seas are less than calm. The process entailed loading the coal into huge bags. The bags were then transferred from the colliers to the Russian warships where they were taken to the bunkers to be emptied. It was a long, hard, labor-intensive effort, and it was effected on the backs of the luckless Russian seamen.

Like Russia, the United States not only lacked the necessary overseas possessions to establish a network of coaling stations, but also lacked a viable merchant marine. To compound the problem, the Navy was short of auxiliaries. In the rush to build a formidable battle fleet, auxiliaries had been virtually ignored. This lack of foresight was aptly pointed out by the former chief of the Bureau of Equipment, Rear Admiral George Melville. Admiral Melville observed that while the Navy was capable of providing defense, its long-range capabilities were woefully inadequate. He pointed to the lack of a homegrown merchant marine. He also offered that since the United States did not enjoy the possession of many overseas territories that the appropriate fleet of colliers and other types of support ships be built. The advantage here was that these were mobile platforms and not static like ports, and therefore less susceptible to capture by an enemy. This, he urged, should be vigorously pursued even at the expense of further battleship construction.

This was sound strategic thinking. It also was ahead of its time, and therefore not appreciated, especially by Congress. Melville's idea would reach fruition in World

War II in the Pacific Theater. Here the fast carrier task forces of the U.S. Pacific Fleet ranged far and wide to smash the Imperial Navy. These formidable strike forces were backed by a large fleet of escort carriers, tankers, and transports, which delivered an unending stream of planes, pilots, spare parts, fuel, and ammunition. Backed by such a support force, the fast carrier task forces could remain at sea almost indefinitely. But that was 1943. In 1907, such an appreciation and application of the strategic principles of sea power was still a generation away.

Another obstacle faced by the president and his planners were the restrictions posed by federal regulations. For the most part, the navy's fuel and supplies were carried on American vessels crewed by American seamen. However, the intrepid Roosevelt was not going to be deterred by the lack of an American merchant marine. If not enough American ships could be made available to cater to the navy's needs, then foreign-flagged carriers would fill the gap.

To stimulate the interest of the American carriers, Roosevelt put an offer on the table, whereby American shippers would be awarded contracts if their bids did not exceed foreign offers by more than fifty percent. Many American carriers declined this offer, mainly because most could not obtain enough freight to cover the cost of the return trip. This was especially true in the Pacific. With little more than two months before the fleet was set to sail, President Roosevelt made a decision. He ordered the Navy Department to procure the services of thirty-eight vessels to supply coal for the fleet for its journey from Hampton Roads to San Francisco. It had been calculated that steaming round South America would consume some 125,000 tons of coal. Of the thirty-eight vessels contracted to carry this coal, only eight would fly the Stars and Stripes.

Most of the thirty foreign-flagged carriers would fly the Union Jack. This development led to a curious strategic conundrum. One of the major aims of the cruise was to impress upon Tokyo the American ability to project overwhelming naval power from the Atlantic to the Pacific in time of crisis. Yet it seemed that the American ability to project long-range power was based on the support of the British merchant marine. Britain, in turn, had a military alliance with Japan since 1905. This obligated Britain to come to aid of its ally if Japan found itself at war with another power. London's primary concern was the growing threat posed by the German Navy. By playing both sides of the fence, London hoped to cool any heat generated by Japanese-American friction. The Imperial Navy could be relied upon to assist the Royal Navy in protection of His Majesty's colonies in the Far East. While in the Atlantic, the burgeoning American fleet could be looked upon for support in the face of the challenge posed by the kaiser's navy. This reliance on proxies underscored the developing shift in dynamics: That being the slow but inexorable eclipse of British hegemony and the rise of Japanese and American power.

"ISN'T IT MAGNIFICENT?"

Sixteen gleaming white battlewagons gathered at the mouth of Hampton Roads. They assembled by squadron, two columns, each parallel to the other. Those of First Battleship Squadron fell astern the flagship *Connecticut*. Second Battleship Squadron lined up aft *Minnesota*. Commander of First Squadron was Rear Admiral Robley D. Evans, while Rear Admiral Charles M. Thomas commanded Second Squadron. Overall task force commander was Robley D. Evans.

"Fightin' Bob Evans," as he was known, was tougher than the armor plate on his flagship. A southerner by birth, he was born in Floyd County, Virginia, on August 18, 1846. He was attending the Naval Academy at Annapolis when the American Civil War broke out in 1861. He graduated in 1863 and was immediately assigned to the fleet.

Early in 1865, a Union invasion fleet gathered off North Carolina. On January 15, Ensign Evans and one hundred sailors and marines from the *Powhaton* stormed ashore. They were joined with other volunteer detachments in an attempt to dislodge stubborn Confederate defenders from Fort Fisher. Out in front of the assault, Evans took a bullet in the thigh. He quickly dressed his wound and threw himself back into the attack. He was leading his section when another slug shattered his knee and a third blew away a toe and mangled his ankle. This time the intrepid ensign was evacuated from the battle area and put aboard the *Santiago de Cuba* bound for Norfolk.

The young ensign was seriously wounded. A surgeon who examined him told him he would die unless his leg was amputated. Evans reached under his pillow and produced a pistol. He warned the surgeon in no uncertain terms that if he returned with a saw he would be shot. Evans pulled through, but he was left with a limp and constant pain for the rest of his life.

Following the southern surrender, the navy discharged Evans as unfit for duty. Robley D. Evans was not a man easily deterred. He wanted back in the service and even lobbied Congress to do it. It took a number of years, but Evans' persistence paid off. He was returned to active duty.

In January 1891, Chile erupted into revolution. Units of the U.S. Navy were assigned to protect American lives and interests. One of the ships sent to Valparaiso was the gunboat *Yorktown*. Her commander was Robley D. Evans. Evans' tough and steady coolness won him accolades when he brokered a tough standoff between Chilean and American bluejackets.

Seven years later, during the Spanish-American War, Captain Robley D. Evans was in command of America's newest and most powerful battleship, the *Iowa*. On May 12, 1898, *Iowa* was among a squadron that engaged in a two-hour slugfest with Spanish shore batteries at San Juan de Puerto Rico. *Iowa* took one hit and had three sailors wounded.

On July 3, *Iowa*, in consort with *Brooklyn, Oregon, Texas, Indiana,* and the light yacht *Gloucester* took on a Spanish task force at Santiago de Cuba. The Spanish

Admiral Pascual Cervera, in his flagship *Infanta Maria Teresa*, led *Vizcaya*, *Cristobal Colon*, *Almirante Oquendo* and the destroyers *Furor* and *Pluton*.

Iowa opened up on the Spanish flagship. Other ships in the American column joined in. American shells screamed in. In less time than it takes to smoke a cigarette, the *Infanta Maria Teresa* took thirty hits. She skidded out of formation, her topsides a shambles. Evans shifted targets to *Vizcaya*. Other Americans ships trained their guns on *Cristobal Colon* and *Almirante Oquendo*. The *Almirante Oquendo* and the luckless *Infanta Maria Teresa* ran aground. *Iowa* continued to press her case against *Vizcaya*, while the rest of the American column took after the fleeing *Cristobal Colon*.

Evans continued his unremitting attack on the doomed *Vizcaya*. Spewing smoke and flame, her guns muted and her topsides wrecked, *Vizcaya* ran aground. Her crew struck her colors and Evans ordered ceasefire. But as the Spanish crewmen abandoned ship, they were set upon by vengeful Cubans. Joined by Lieutenant-Commander Wainwright of *Gloucester*, Evans ordered landing parties ashore to protect the helpless Spanish sailors. Evans went so far as to threaten the Cubans with bombardment if they did not cease their attacks.

Vizcaya's Captain Eulante and 271 crewmen were rescued. The wounded were cared for and five Spanish dead were buried with full honors. Meanwhile, Evans and his command had served with distinction. Of personal note for Captain Evans was that his son, too, was serving aboard *Iowa* as a fresh cadet.

Over the next nine years, Evans worked his way up to flag rank. When it came time to pick a commander for the

Great White Fleet, none was more qualified than Rear Admiral Robley D. Evans. But the damage incurred by Evans' body had taken its toll. By December 16, 1907, he was suffering from rheumatic gout. His condition steadily worsened as the Great White Fleet sailed on. Wracked with constant pain, Evans was eventually relegated to bed. Try as he might, not even the stalwart Evans could deny the inevitable. He was relieved of command before the fleet made its triumphal entry into San Francisco.

Evans' flagship was the battleship *Connecticut*. *Connecticut* was the latest and best that America had to offer. She was the lead ship of a class of six, the largest single class of battleships ever produced by the United States. The *Connecticuts* displaced 17,650 tons at full load and had a top speed of eighteen knots. They mounted four twelve-inch, eight eight-inch, and twelve seven-inch main batteries. Five of the sixteen battleships of the Great White Fleet were from the *Connecticut* class—*Connecticut, Louisiana, Vermont, Kansas,* and *Minnesota.* The sixth, *New Hampshire,* was not commissioned until March 19, 1908, and therefore missed the cruise. The *Connecticuts* were the epitome of American pre-dreadnought design. They were among the last of an era as the Royal Navy's *Dreadnought*, with her faster speed, thicker armor, and greater firepower, rendered the *Connecticuts* and every other pre-dreadnought in the world obsolete. The United States made the jump to the dreadnought type as well, with the *South Carolina* and *Michigan.* They were commissioned into the fleet in 1910.

Next came four of the five *Virginia* class. These

mounted four twelve-inch, eight eight-inch, and twelve six-inch main armament. Fully loaded they displaced 16,094 tons and had a top speed of eighteen knots. They were as follows: *Virginia, Georgia, New Jersey,* and *Rhode Island.*

The *Maine* class was represented by the *Maine, Missouri,* and *Ohio.* The *Maines* mounted four twelve-inch and sixteen six-inch main batteries. They tipped the scales at 13,500 tons at full load and had a top speed of eighteen knots.

Illinois and *Alabama* represented the *Illinois* class. These battleships mounted four thirteen-inch and fourteen six-inch main armament. They weighed 12,150 tons fully loaded and had a top speed of sixteen knots.

The last two ships were the oldest, having been launched in March 1898. These were the *Kearsarge* and *Kentucky.* Each mounted four thirteen-inch, four eight-inch, and fourteen five-inch main batteries. Each displaced 12,320 tons at full load and had a top speed of sixteen knots.

Kearsarge is of particular interest, as it was the only American battleship not named for a state. She was so-named by Act of Congress in commemoration of the Union man-of-war that hunted down the famous Confederate raider *Alabama* during the Civil War. *Kearsarge* would go on to enjoy the longest term of uninterrupted service by any battleship in American history.

Kearsarge was launched on March 24, 1898, and commissioned on February 20, 1900. *Kearsarge* served as an active duty battleship until August 20, 1920. She was then converted to a crane ship and designated AB-1. It was *Kearsarge* that raised the ill-fated submarine *Squalus* in 1939. On November 6, 1941, the name *Kearsarge* was transferred to one of the *Essex* class aircraft carriers then under construction. AB-1 continued in her capacity as a crane ship for another fourteen years. She was struck from the Navy roster on June 22, 1955, and sold for scrap on August 9, 1955, after fifty-five years of continuous service.

For more than a week before the day of departure, Roosevelt's battlewagons began to mass off Old Point Comfort. Ashore, Hampton Roads became a Mecca for merrymakers, curiosity seekers, and patriots. They filled every hotel, inn, and roadhouse, countless thousands of them, eager and excited to witness the sailing of so powerful an American fleet. Yet amid the euphoria there occurred an episode of racial injustice. An action taken by the Navy which, based on the general American fear of the "Yellow Peril," forecast an even greater injustice that was to befall Japanese-Americans more than thirty years later.

Since the mid 1890s, Asians had joined the navy in a variety of noncombatant roles, such as cooks and valets. Many of these were Japanese. In an era of antipathy toward the Japanese, many naval officers thought it inadvisable to allow Japanese to serve on board American warships, especially if the fleet ever had to come to grips with the Imperial Navy. One of the most ardent champions of the cause was Rear Admiral Albert S. Barker.

Admiral Barker began his naval career during the Civil War. In 1874, while assigned to the Navy's Torpedo Station at Newport, Rhode Island, Barker was reputed to be the first American to fire high explosive shells. Barker later commanded the cruiser *Newark* during the Spanish-American War. In 1903, Admiral Barker was named commander-in-chief of the Atlantic Fleet, a post he held for two years.

During the planning stages of the Great White Fleet, Admiral Dewey of Manila Bay fame sought Barker's advice on the possibility of war with Japan. One of Barker's suggestions was that the navy should rid itself of its Japanese auxiliaries or reassign them to duties ashore. The fact that none of these people had never engaged in subversive activities of any kind made no difference.

Yet the decision was made and the Japanese auxiliaries were put ashore. Despite the indignity, every one of them obeyed their orders to the letter. It was an episode starkly prophetic of the mass relocation of Japanese-Americans after the Imperial Navy's surprise attack on Pearl Harbor in December 1941.

The plight of the noncombatants did nothing to mar the festivities planned for the officers and men of the Great White Fleet. It was known as Navy Farewell Week and it began on December 9. For the next six days, receptions, teas, luncheons, balls, and parties were thrown with round-the-clock regularity. The highlight celebration was on Friday, December 13, at the Chamberlin Hotel. Admiral Evans and the officers of the Great White Fleet were feted by many of the nation's upper crust. From Washington, Richmond, Baltimore, Norfolk, and other cities up and down the East Coast, came the wealthy, all looking to be associated in one way or another with the great enterprise.

The weather soured on Saturday and Sunday and

Hampton Roads was drenched in heavy rains. But the soaking did nothing to dampen spirits. And on Monday, December 16, the day of departure, dawned sunny and bright.

At 0800 hours, the fleet greeted the new day with morning colors. Ashore the anticipation of the army of onlookers was at fever pitch. The excitement of the moment was felt by those in the fleet as well. Every ship was bedecked in flags and pennants. Sailors and marines in dress whites and blues manned the railings. Bands blared from the quarter deck of every ship, all in anticipation of the president's review. On signal from the flagship, the entire squadron loosed a twenty-one-gun salute in deference to the commander-in-chief. This was the signal for the *Mayflower* to begin the review. The presidential yacht began to make its way slowly between the two columns of floating steel fortresses. After he had acknowledged several of the ships, President Roosevelt, excited and overwhelmed by the moment, turned to Secretary of the Navy Metcalf and marveled, "Did you ever see such a fleet? Isn't it magnificent?"

Mayflower approached Fort Monroe. The bastion's gunners boomed out a salute to the president's flag. At the mouth of the Roads, the presidential yacht dropped anchor. Barges and gigs shuttled flag officers and battleship skippers to the *Mayflower*. President Roosevelt took the time to pose for photographs and chat with each and every one of them. The president concluded the reception by meeting privately first with Admiral Evans and then with second-in-command, Admiral Thomas.

The officers were shuttled back to their commands. The presidential yacht got under way and proceeded slowly into Chesapeake Bay. On signal from the flagship, anchor chains began to clatter noisily against armor plate. Props began to churn the waters off Old Point Comfort. Funnels began to belch plumes of thick black smoke. At the head of First Battleship Squadron, *Connecticut* pointed her prow seaward. Second Battleship Squadron fell astern the First, as the great white line of warships snaked its way out of the Roads. On the quarter deck of *Connecticut*, the ship's band played "Auld Lang Syne" to the cheering masses ashore.

Mayflower waited off Tail-of-the-Horseshoe-Lightship. The Great White Fleet steamed out of Chesapeake Bay for the final presidential review. Evans' ships were spaced four hundred yards apart in a column that stretched for three miles. As each ship passed in review, officers were arrayed on deck, and bluejackets and marines stood stiffly on parade. Each battleship fired a twenty-one-gun salute to the commander-in-chief.

It originally had been planned for the presidential yacht to return to the nation's capital following the final review. But an exuberant president ordered *Mayflower's* captain to continue to shadow the fleet. This he did until the Virginia Capes. Here *Mayflower* pulled abreast *Connecticut*. President Roosevelt bid farewell to his magnificent fleet of sixteen first-line battleships and the 14,500 officers and men who manned them. *Mayflower* then broke off and turned for home. The Great White Fleet slowly melted into the distance. Theodore Roosevelt, tight-lipped and silent, stared out at the horizon until all that remained of his fleet was a wisp of black smoke.

Evans' battleships sailed out of Chesapeake Bay in single-line formation. This was the preferred mode of steaming in restricted waters. Once out into the open sea, the fleet broke down into squadrons or divisions. These smaller formations enabled a task force to respond more quickly to flag signals and enable a commander to maneuver his ships as a unit more efficiently than in a single column.

Off Cape Hatteras, Admiral Evans redeployed his fleet into divisions. Each division was a four-ship column, and each column steamed in parallel to the other at a distance of 1,600 yards. In each column, ships maintained intervals of four hundred yards.

Rear Admiral Robley D. Evans was a man of many hats. First and foremost he was task force commander. He also was commander of First Battleship Squadron as well as First Battleship Division. *Connecticut*, proudly flying Evans' flag, led First Division, followed by *Kansas*, *Vermont*, and *Louisiana*. Second Division was commanded by Rear Admiral William H. Emory, flying his flag aboard *Georgia*. Steaming aft were *New Jersey*, *Rhode Island*, and *Virginia*. Evans' deputy commander, Rear Admiral Charles M. Thomas, commanded Second Battleship Squadron as well as Third Battleship Division. Thomas flew his flag aboard *Minnesota*, trailed in turn by *Ohio*, *Missouri*, and *Maine*. Rear Admiral Charles S. Sperry commanded Fourth Battleship Division, flying his flag aboard *Alabama*. Astern lumbered *Illinois*, *Kearsarge*, and *Kentucky*.

Throughout the ships, the rumor mills were working overtime. Speculation as to the fleet's destination was the hot topic of the day. The riddle was cleared up after dinner on the first night at sea. Over the wireless, Rear

Admiral Evans announced to his command, "The president has authorized the commander-in-chief to inform the officers and men that after a short stay on the Pacific coast, it is the president's intention to have the fleet return to the Atlantic coast by way of the Mediterranean."

Evans' matter-of-fact pronouncement had an effect all out of proportion to the brief Navy English with which it had been composed. It was a bombshell. A round-the-world cruise! Nothing like it before had been attempted on such a scale! Just think of it, sixteen battleships sailing round the world!

However, unbeknownst to Admiral Evans, his signal had been picked up ashore. Soon the intention of his fleet was emblazoned on the headlines of the nation's newspapers. The White House quickly issued a denial. Secretary of the Navy Victor Metcalf stated that the fleet would round South America on its way to San Francisco. How it would return home had yet to be determined.

While Washington scrambled to address the public relations gaffe, the incident served to show the profound effect that the new wonder of communication was going to have on the handling of ships at sea. The wireless transmission enabled a task force commander to issue orders in real-world time, providing an instantaneous advantage over whistle, flag, and horn. The wireless also put the task force commander in contact with his superiors ashore. This development would prove a double-edged sword. On the upside, the task force commander could now obtain the latest in military and political intelligence that could assist him in how best to employ his ships. The downside was that those higher up the chain of command could now restrict the task force commander's freedom of action if they chose to do so.

The wireless would forever alter the conduct of sea power. However, it could not change the aim of sea power. Control of the seas was still the aim of sea power. For the United States Navy, command of the seas depended on the success or failure of the Great White Fleet. It was imperative that Evans' task force impress the American people and demonstrate to them the importance of the fleet to their security. At the same time, the Navy Department sought to justify to Congress that the money spent on building up the battleship force was indeed money well spent. If, like the ill-fated Russian Baltic Fleet, the American ships and crews proved unequal to the task, then the endeavor could be ended at San Francisco, hopefully without too much embarrassment. This meant that there would be no more public pronouncements as to the fleet's ultimate destination until its arrival in San Francisco.

Yet none of this mattered to the crews of the sixteen American battleships. For many of them, they were on their way to the greatest adventure of their lives. For the nation, its standing and prestige in the world were at stake. For the navy, success or failure would almost certainly decide its future with Congress and the American people. For better or for worse, America's bid to become a global power rode the decks of the Great White Fleet.

"END OF THE WORLD!"

On December 20, the fleet was off Puerto Rico. And already shades of the Russian Baltic Fleet were beginning to cast a pall over Roosevelt's task force. *Kentucky* dropped out due to engineering problems. Two hours later, *Illinois* fell out. The former effected repairs and quickly resumed station. The latter, upon completion of repairs, steamed for Culebra to put ashore a seaman who had fallen ill. The *Missouri* detached and sped for San Juan to put ashore a bluejacket who had taken sick. Both ships rejoined the fleet the following day in the Virgin Passage.

On December 22, the Great White Fleet suffered its first fatality, ordinary seaman Robert Eugenpipes of *Alabama.* The sailor had succumbed to pneumonia and spinal meningitis. His body was committed to the Caribbean Sea. The next day, a lookout spotted a white lighthouse.

The fleet had reached the Gulf of Paria. The gateway to the Gulf was known as the *Bocas del Dragon,* or the Dragon's Mouth. The Dragon's Mouth is a twelve-mile channel and is a minefield of rocky islets and outcrops waiting to rip open the stoutest armor plate like tissue paper. Admiral Evans arranged his ships into a single-line formation. Astern *Connecticut,* the column snaked its way through the treacherous waterway. Not one ship so much as even scratched the paint as the fleet broke into the Gulf.

The Gulf of Paria was known originally as the *Golfo de la Ballena* (the Gulf of the Whale). It is a shallow inland sea of three thousand square miles. It was discovered by Columbus during the famed explorer's third voyage to the New World. The Gulf of Paria is considered one of the finest natural harbors in the world. It connects the Caribbean Sea to the north with the Atlantic Ocean to the south. To the west lies Venezuela and to the east is Trinidad. As its original name implies, the Gulf was once a habitat rich with whales, but unrestricted hunting had so decimated the herds that by the nineteenth century the whale populations never recovered.

Connecticut led the column across the Gulf of Paria to Port-of-Spain. Outside the harbor, the fleet conducted an elaborate maneuver. On signal from the flagship, First Battleship Division swung sharply ninety degrees. Each division followed suit, executing the turn to starboard with flawless precision. "It was," Admiral Evans later observed, "the finest naval sight ever witnessed."[1]

Waiting in the harbor was a flotilla of torpedo-boats. These lightweights of the fleet had left Hampton Roads two weeks ahead of the battleships. Joining them were five naval auxiliaries and five colliers loaded to the gunnels with coal. That evening thirty-two American vessels rode at anchor in the harbor. Port-of-Spain looked more like an American naval base than a British possession.

The Great White Fleet's first major visit did not start off well, and the culprit was British intransigence. The British governor, Sir Henry Moore Jackson, was scheduled to receive Admiral Evans the morning following the fleet's arrival. Protocol dictated that the British governor reciprocate Evans' visit with one of his own aboard

Connecticut. However, Jackson sent word that he would pay his respects to Admiral Evans and his entourage ashore at the Queen's Park Hotel. This affront could not have come at a worse time for Admiral Evans. His rheumatic gout had progressed to the point where he could no longer walk. He was now totally dependent upon the assistance of two aides; however, the indignities did not end there. When the admiral's gig tied up at the dock, instead of the customary honor guard, Evans' official greeting consisted of a few policemen and musicians from the local constabulary.

Contempt of protocol was just the beginning of Sir Henry's indiscretions. The British business community of Port-of-Spain had planned a ball for American officers. Sir Henry persuaded them to cancel their plans, saying that his office would arrange the affair. Nothing was done. Then there was the debacle involving the British Navy's plan for a reception for the officers of the Great White Fleet. Two-hundred and fifty invitations were sent. Admirals Evans, Sperry, Thomas, and Emory attended, together with their adjutants. None of the other officers of the fleet bothered to show up. This embarrassment was corrected for the rest of the cruise. From there on out, all officers would be required to attend such social functions.

The reason for British coolness to the American visit was based, in part, out of concern for the Anglo-Japanese Alliance. London did not want Tokyo to get the impression that it was cozying up to Washington. After all, both Britain and the United States were Caucasian, Christian countries. There was also the long-simmering Tory distaste for the colonies and its distrust of American intentions. For, by 1907, much of the Royal Navy had been withdrawn to home waters to face the growing German naval threat. This left His Majesty's possessions in the West Indies virtually unprotected. British concerns for their Caribbean interests were underscored by an incident that had occurred earlier in the year. This was known as the Swettenham-Davis Affair.

On January 15, 1907, Jamaica was rocked by an earthquake. Hundreds were killed. Damage was extensive and fires raged out of control. At Guantanamo Bay, American Rear Admiral Davis got word of the disaster. With two battleships and a destroyer, he rushed to the scene.

When Admiral Davis entered Jamaica harbor, he failed to acknowledge the Union Jack. British Colonial-Governor Sir Alexander Swettenham took offense to the Yankee officer's flagrant disregard for protocol. But Admiral Davis either forgot or ignored accepted protocol in an effort to commence relief efforts as quickly as possible. He dropped anchor and sent a large party of sailors and marines ashore. Despite the fact that the landing party was there for humanitarian assistance only, Governor Swettenham interpreted American actions as an unwarranted intrusion. He demanded the immediate withdrawal of the American contingent. He also wired London and Washington, expressing his displeasure at the so-called American intervention. The issue quickly blossomed into an international incident, as the press on both sides of the Atlantic fanned the flames of nationalism.

In the end, Sir Alexander Swettenham resigned. And the incident caused a fraying of the nerves between Washington and London. For the British, the embarrassment of having a foreign navy render assistance to a possession of the Crown cut very deeply. But with only a single warship available between Bermuda and Georgetown, there was really not much else that could be done.

The major fallout from the Swettenham-Davis Affair had largely dissipated by the time of the Great White Fleet's arrival at Port-of-Spain in December. But the lingering effects were obvious judging by Governor Jackson's treatment of the hobbled American admiral. However, Evans would have the last laugh. For when the impudent British governor looked out his window across the harbor, he would see more than thirty vessels riding at anchor and all would be flying the Stars and Stripes.

In the overall scheme of things, the importance of the Swettenham-Davis Affair meant very little. The main reason for the American presence in Port-of-Spain was to coal. Those members of the crews not assigned to coaling detail enjoyed liberty. Some stayed on board their ships, while others went ashore. Those who went ashore took in the sights, rode the trolleys, or got up baseball games.

Shipboard entertainment took on many forms. There were concerts, minstrel shows, boxing, singing, vaudeville acts, boating, and boat races. It is important to remember that in 1907, there were no radios, TVs, videos, or DVD players. The turn-of-the-century American bluejacket enjoyed the much-simpler forms of entertainment and was quite adept at keeping himself amused. This was especially true on the holidays. Christmas Day was spent in Trinidad. Sailors and officers decorated their ships. Buddies exchanged gifts. Cards and letters from home were read and shared with shipmates. In each section of each ship, Christmas dinner was provided for the crew. A contingent of officers went from ship to ship caroling the night away.

December 29 was the scheduled day of departure. Every ship had been fueled and provisioned, yet coal could prove to be a problem for the next leg of the cruise. It was only 1,800 miles from Hampton Roads to Trinidad. But it was 3,400 miles to the next port-of-call, Rio de Janeiro. For battleships of the *Virginia* and *Connecticut* classes, the steam to Rio would not be a problem. But *Illinois* and *Alabama* were older ships with smaller bunker capacities, while *Maine* and *New Jersey* seemed to have developed voracious appetites for coal. So the order came down. The fleet would steam at no more than ten knots. On *Illinois, Alabama, Maine,* and *New Jersey,* luxuries such as bathing and the use of electric lights would have to be rationed in an effort to conserve coal. After all, no one wanted to endure the embarrassment of having his ship towed into port.

After crude oil, the most commonly traded commodity in the world is coffee. It joins tea and tap water as the world's three most ingested beverages. The leading exporter of coffee is Brazil. In 1908, the importance of coffee to American-Brazilian relations can be understood by a simple equation: Coffee was Brazil's number one export, and the United States was Brazil's number one customer.

While most of South America was culturally and ethnically tied to Spain, Brazil was not. Brazil was originally colonized by the Portuguese, and as such, Portuguese was the official language of the country. During the nineteenth and early twentieth centuries, immigrants poured into Brazil. Many came from Europe. Some came from Asia. At the same time that Brazil was ingesting this flood of humanity, she was industrializing. By the beginning of the twentieth century, Brazil was a young, up-and-coming power like the United States.

Landwise, Brazil is the largest nation in South America and the fifth largest on the globe. At 3,300,169 square miles, she is nearly as large as China. Brazil's strategic importance is evidenced by her coastline, which commands much of the South Atlantic. This coastline would prove invaluable in two World Wars. This was especially true in World War II, when bases along Brazil's coast proved decisive in combating the U-boat menace. It was no wonder then that when the Great White Fleet came to call, the Brazilians enthusiastically greeted the Americans as equals among the important powers of the New World.

At 1600 hours on December 29, 1907, the American battleships steamed out of Port-of-Spain. *Connecticut* led the way out of the Gulf of Paria, through the Dragon's Mouth, and into the Caribbean Sea. The fleet rounded Trinidad and headed south into the Atlantic. The fleet was expected to arrive at Rio de Janeiro on January 12, this having been revised upwards from the 10th. The delay was owing to several engineering mishaps and to *Missouri*, which had lost a man overboard. However, a strong southerly current was helping to push the fleet along at eleven knots. This was good news for *Illinois, Alabama, Maine,* and *New Jersey.* These ships would make Rio with coal with spare.

At 0930, on the morning of January 12, the Brazilian naval escort moved out to meet the American fleet. Evans' task force was reported off Cape Frio, some seventy miles to the north. The Brazilian escort met the Yankee battle-ships off Guanabara Harbor. The cruiser *Barroso* fired a fifteen-gun salute to Admiral Evans' flag. Then the escort fell into the American formation. As the ships passed Fort Villagagnon, *Connecticut* loosed a twenty-one-gun salute to Brazil. The multitude ashore waved and cheered as the Brazilian battleship *Florian* boomed out a thirteen-gun reply. This was followed by another thunderous salute from the German cruiser *Bremen*.

The warmth and hospitality of Rio was in stark con-trast to the chilly atmosphere of Port-of-Spain. Respects were paid to the ailing Admiral Evans straightway. All the American flag officers and battleship skippers were assem-bled aboard *Connecticut*. Joining them were the American consul, Brazil's Minister of Marine, the port captain of Rio, numerous commandants from the Brazilian Navy, and members of the official welcoming committee and local civic authorities. Unlike at Port-of-Spain, all American officers would be required to attend the social functions planned by their gracious Brazilian hosts. That is, all save Admiral Evans, who by now was a cripple. Rear Admiral Charles M. Thomas, second in command, would stand in for Admiral Evans in all aspects of the commander-in-chief for the duration of the visit.

Diplomatic protocol is an important function for a naval officer. In standing in for Admiral Evans, Admiral Thomas, with Admirals Emory and Sperry and all bat-tleship skippers, spent the next couple of days attending one diplomatic function after another. They first visited the Minister of Marine in Rio. Then they adjourned to Thomas' flagship *Minnesota*, where the minister returned the favor. Then they boarded a train for the twenty-mile ride to the Petropolis, Brazil's summer capital, for an audience with President Penna. Afterwards they attended a banquet given at the residence of the American ambassador. Here they spent the night. The next morning they took the train back to Rio to attend a luncheon given by the Minister of Marine.

For the enlisted personnel, the situation was much less formal. Yet it was no less important, because officer and rating alike was expected to represent the United States in a favorable light. This meant keeping the bluejackets and leathernecks busy. The American community, with assistance from the British community and Brazilian authorities, planned a series of functions. Dances, games, concerts, and tours all made the American visit a rousing success. Not even the mass waterfront brawl on the first night ashore spoiled the success of this port-of-call. In fact, because of the visit of the Great White Fleet, U.S.-Brazilian relations emerged stronger than ever.

Yet it was not all fun and games, for there was still the tedium of coaling. Ships took turns replenishing their bunkers. This time the colliers supplying the coal were from the navy. Therein lay the problem. In an effort to get to Rio without running out of fuel, the crews of the colliers had to pinch some of the fleet's coal. This left Evans short over three thousand tons. It also left him short of patience. He shot off a wireless to the Navy Department. He explained that the current type of navy collier was adequate for short-range operations. But for extended operations, it was a dismal failure. Again the lack of auxiliaries and a viable merchant marine served to underscore America's weakness as a naval power. Fortunately, Evans' fleet was scheduled to take on coal at its next stop, Punta Arenas, Chile.

Meanwhile, another problem arose: Argentina. Argentina had been scratched off the fleet's itinerary. This caused a big flap in Buenos Aires, for Argentina and Brazil were competing regional powers and were not on the best of terms. And the blossoming U.S.-Brazilian relationship was viewed in Buenos Aires with the greatest suspicion.

This was not the first time Argentina felt slighted. In 1907, a U.S. cruiser squadron had put into Rio. During the Jamestown Exposition, the visiting Brazilian delegation was given the red carpet treatment at the White House. Argentine misgivings were further inflamed when Brazil placed an order for several dreadnought battleships with British shipyards. Buenos Aires saw this as nothing less than an attempt to establish naval supremacy in the South Atlantic. In an effort to address the fleet imbalance, Argentina placed her own order for British battleships. Yet this was in direct contravention with its treaty with Chile, which placed limitations on warship construction.

The fleet's itinerary caused a blizzard of signals to be exchanged between Buenos Aires, the U.S. Embassy in Brazil, and Washington. Yet no amount of wrangling could change the fact that it was physically impossible for the American battleships to put into Buenos Aires. The waters of the Argentine capital were just too shallow. This prompted a compromise. In agreement with Admiral Evans, Lieutenant Hutchinson I. Cone's torpedo-boat flotilla would detach itself from the fleet and proceed to Argentina. The scheduled visit to Montevideo, Uruguay, was scrubbed. Cone's squadron would sail up the Rio del Plata for Buenos Aires. Following the visit, the flotilla was to proceed to Punta Arenas and rendezvous with Evans' battleships.

At 20:30 hours on January 21, the torpedo-boat destroyers *Lawrence, Hull, Hopkins, Stewart, Whipple,* and *Truxton* departed Rio for Buenos Aires. They arrived early on the morning of the 26th. The visiting bluejackets were treated like royalty. Destroyer skippers with the rank of lieutenant were treated like admirals, attending official functions hosted by the American legation, the Argentine Minister of Marine, and even the Argentine president. For the moment at least, the earlier political row had been forgotten.

The battleships departed Rio on January 22, the day after the torpedo-boat flotilla. Aboard the presidential yacht, *Silva Jardin,* was President Penna, the American ambassador, and a host of Brazilian dignitaries. As the presidential yacht reviewed the fleet, the battleships boomed out a twenty-one-gun salute. President Penna came aboard the *Minnesota* and was received by Admiral Thomas. Following a short reception, President Penna returned to the *Silva Jardin.* The presidential yacht proceeded to a point just off Fort Villagagnon for a final review of the fleet.

The battleships steamed out of Rio in single file. The rain was coming down in buckets, but thousands of Brazilians braved the downpour to see the fleet off. They were treated to a thunderous barrage as American guns rendered salutes to Fort Villagagnon and the *Silva Jardin.* The cannonading marked the end of the visit, a visit that proved highly successful for both nations. Yet in many of the analyses of the visits made by the American fleet during the round-the-world cruise, one intriguing aspect is almost always overlooked. And in the case of Brazil, it was the root of success: how the host viewed his American visitor. From the commander-in-chief on down to the lowliest rating, the American sailor was held in high regard and got on famously with his Brazilian host. This is because the typical American sailor was the product of a society that, for the most part, seemed to imbue in its young people the virtues of decency and fair play, attributes of which America was formerly renowned. The young American sailor, then, was not looked upon as representing a military threat, but as an ambassador of American values. Whether in dress whites or blues, the American sailor was just the common everyday Joe inter-acting with the common everyday Joe of the country he was visiting. And it is just such an interaction between the peoples of two nations that always bears a far richer fruit than can ever be harvested from relations carried on at the diplomatic level. This is what was reflected the next day in the Brazilian press, which trumpeted its pro-American stance by alluding to the possibility of an alliance between the two up-and-coming giants of the New World.

Once out in the open sea, the fleet broke into divisions. The next leg was 2,374 miles. But the fleet would not have to make the entire journey alone. Filtering out of the Rio del Plata on a course of interception was the Argentine San Martin Division. It featured the cruisers *San Martin, Buenos Ayres, Pueyrredon,* and *9 de Julio,* all under the command of Rear Admiral Hipolito Oliva.

On the evening of the 26th, the searchlights of the Great White Fleet were turned skyward and switched on.

Oliva's cruisers homed in on the beacon and found the American task force. Oliva traded greetings with Admiral Evans, after which the Argentine warships fell astern the American formation.

At daybreak, Evans' battleships formed a single column astern *Connecticut*. The Argentine cruisers drew abreast along the starboard side, their bands playing the "Star-Spangled Banner." Oliva's flagship, *San Martin*, drew abeam *Connecticut*. An American ensign shot up the Argentine's yardarm and a seventeen-gun salute thundered across the South Atlantic. Aboard *Connecticut*, the Argentine flag was hoisted and a reciprocating broadside roared out in reply.

Final signals of goodwill were exchanged and the Argentine cruisers peeled off for home. The Great White Fleet continued south, on its way toward one of the most famous waterways in the world, the Strait of Magellan.

The Strait of Magellan severs mainland South America from Tierra del Fuego. Named for Ferdinand Magellan, who sailed through it in 1520, the circuitous waterway is 330 miles long and from two to fifteen miles wide. The strait provides a more palatable route of passage from the Atlantic to the Pacific, to the more tempestuous waters of the Drake Passage south of Cape Horn.

Yet the Strait of Magellan is fraught with navigational hazards of its own. The climate is inhospitable and, for much of the time, socked in by fog. It is strewn with bottlenecks that can slow progress to a crawl. And then there is the occasional minefield of obstacles, such as rocky outcrops waiting to tear the bottom out of the unwary ship.

Late in the afternoon of January 31, 1908, the Great White Fleet rounded the tip of Patagonia and issued into Possession Bay. The Americans were at the gateway of the Strait of Magellan. Here the ships dropped anchor for the night. Signal Officer Louis Maxfield gazed at the cold, lonely barren landscape, and said, "We seem to be at the end of the world."[2]

At 0330 hours the following morning, *Connecticut* preceded the task force into the straits. In single-line formation, the column snaked its way through the narrows. About midday, the ships entered Broad Reach, the bay to Punta Arenas. Thousands of Chileans lined the ragged coastline. *Connecticut,* flying a Chilean flag, fired a twenty-one-gun salute to Rear Admiral Juan M. Simpson aboard the cruiser *Chacabuco.* Riding at anchor was His Majesty's cruiser HMS *Sappho.* The British man-of-war fired a salute to Admiral Evans' flag.

The American ships were ushered into the harbor and there berthed by squadron. The first part of the journey was over. They were halfway to San Francisco. Apart from the crippled Admiral Evans, there had been no major setbacks. Not one ship had dropped out. Teddy Roosevelt's battle fleet had reached the end of the world.

"VIVA LOS YANKEES!"

Connecticut's engines were not even cold when Admiral Simpson's chief-of-staff was piped aboard. He reported directly to Admiral Evans. He informed the bedridden commander-in-chief that Admiral Simpson would soon be calling to issue an official welcome. The friendly, even eager greeting seemed out of character for a nation that had, at best, a guarded view of the United States.

To many Chileans, the growing power of the United States was a mixed blessing. As champion of the Monroe Doctrine, the United States had put an end to centuries of colonial rule by Spain. At the same time, the United States was seen as the new bully on the block. Victory in the Spanish-American War had enabled the United States to seize the Philippines, Guam, and Puerto Rico. In 1903, Washington coerced the Columbians and Panamanians to secure the rights for the Canal. While closer to home, there was the widely held belief among Chileans that their powerful neighbor to the north had meddled in their internal affairs during a time of national crisis. This was known as the *Baltimore Incident*.

In 1891, Chile was in the throes of civil war. Those fighting to overthrow the government needed arms. One such source was the United States. In California, a steamer was loaded with guns and ammunition for the rebels. But Washington infuriated the revolutionaries by seizing the steamer en route. Regardless, the rebels triumphed in the end, but they never forgave Washington for "meddling in Chile's internal affairs."

If the Americans had short memories, the Chileans did not. Later that year, the cruiser *Baltimore* had put into Valparaiso. News of the ship's arrival spread through the city like a plague. Trouble quickly ensued, as mobs of enraged Chileans attacked U.S. sailors on leave. Two were killed and seventeen were injured. Washington issued a formal protest. The new government in Valparaiso apologized and paid an indemnity of $75,000.

Yet none of this animosity was visible in Punta Arenas. Around the town, American and Chilean flags were thicker than flies. Yet flags and bunting could not hide the spartanness of Punta Arenas. A great forest fire had consumed most of the trees, leaving a scarred and desolate landscape of scorched earth and burned-out trunks. Ramshackle buildings of adobe and brick adorned the waterfront, lending to the cold grimness of the hardscrabble little town of fourteen thousand.

Punta Arenas did not offer much to sailors who were far away from home. There was little in the way of social life. And the stores and gift shops that opened their doors to the sailors and marines had special prices in honor of their visit; that is, the prices were higher than normal. Many of those who were granted liberty chose instead to go hiking or explore the barren landscape. Others crossed the harbor for the hunting expeditions on Tierra del Fuego. For the officers, there were the obligatory social functions. The most lavish was a dinner hosted by the American consul.

One thing Punta Arenas had in abundance was spies. The ships of many nations plied the waters of the Strait of Magellan. Many of these ships called on Punta Arenas, providing ample opportunity for foreign agents to collect intelligence. The Japanese had a team of four spying on the American ships. They observed the fleet from vantage points in the hills overlooking the town. They kept to themselves and were nearly invisible as they conducted their surveillance. Not so the Russians, who had assigned a pair of undercover men who tipped their hand early. These two nincompoops caused a rumpus while trying to board one of the battleships in an effort to get a better look. Yet none was more subtle than the skipper of the HMS *Soppho*, an officer with an engaging personality who was always circulating the social gatherings. Though he got on well with his American counterparts, it was generally agreed that his mingling was for intelligence-gathering purposes.

The main reason for the American stopover was to coal. The run down from Rio was nearly 2,400 miles. The next stop, Lima, was 2,800 miles. This meant that the fleet had enough coal for a slight detour. Admiral Evans received a wireless from the State Department requesting that he take his fleet on a sail-by at Valparaiso. This was to honor a petition from the Chilean Government. In an effort to foster better relations, the diplomatic corps had convinced the White House that it was a good idea. Admiral Evans agreed. On the way to Peru, his ships would put on a demonstration at Valparaiso.

On the final evening of the fleet's visit, Admiral Thomas, pinch-hitting for Admiral Evans, hosted a dinner aboard his flagship *Minnesota* for Chilean dignitaries. Along the shore, thousands had gathered for one last look at their powerful visitors. For them, the navy had a wonderful treat in store. The searchlights of the fleet were turned skyward and switched on. The heavens were lit in a dazzling display to the delight of the onlookers ashore.

The next day, February 7, was the day of departure. The torpedo-boat flotilla, which had arrived three days before, took up escort on either side of the battleships. The battleships were in single file, four hundred yards apart, with eight hundred yards between divisions. *Chacabuco* led the way, with *Connecticut* in her wake. It was 2300 hours. This departure time was chosen so as to allow the fleet to reach Cape Froward by sun up. From there, the run to the sea could be made in complete daylight.

The fleet made it to Cape Pillar without incident. One by one, the ships filtered out of the Strait of Magellan and into the Pacific. Once out into the open sea, the fleet changed course and headed north and ran into a thick bank of fog.

Fog is one of the most hazardous conditions to be encountered at sea. It was crucial that each ship in the task force maintain its station to avoid collision. This meant that each ship had to be constantly aware of the vessels around it. Four means of communication made this possible: Flag, searchlight, steam whistle, and spar. The last-named was also known as a chip log. The chip log was towed astern. The wake or spray it churned up provided the trailing vessel with an unmistakable marker by which it could safely maintain its position.

On the 13th, the curtain of murk began to lift. At the same time, the *Chacabuco* rejoined the fleet. The cruiser had detached the day before and proceeded to Talcahuana to take on more coal. She returned with three destroyers. This was the Chilean escort that would see the Great White Fleet into Valparaiso.

More than a quarter million people had gathered on the hills and beaches of Valparaiso. Riding at anchor in the harbor was the training ship, *General Baquedano*. Aboard was President Pedro Montt, accompanied by Chilean military officers, government officials, and foreign dignitaries. Atop a hill overlooking the scene were five hundred Chilean sailors, clad in dress whites, standing at attention while spelling the word *Welcome*. The greeting was clearly visible from two miles away.

It was nearly noon when the first onlookers spotted the fleet. The ships first appeared as fuzzy plumes of gray black smoke, then poked out of the murkiness to become sparkling white steel fortresses cutting invincibly through the sea. *Connecticut* led the column. Each ship entered the harbor with sailors and marines on parade and flying the Chilean flag.

The American ships rounded the semi-circle of the harbor. When half the column had passed Fort Angeles, the main batteries boomed out a twenty-one-gun salute. *Connecticut*, meanwhile, was plunging past the *General Baquedano*, making for the northern entrance at eight knots. Her sailors and marines on deck snapped to attention as the ship's band struck up the Chilean National Anthem. At the same time, the flagship loosed another twenty-one-gun salute to President Montt.

President Montt acknowledged all sixteen gun salutes. The half-moon of warships rounded the harbor in perfect formation to the approval of the viewers ashore. The caboose of the column was *Kentucky*. As soon as the battlewagon slid past the *General Baquedano*, the fleet upped speed another two knots. On signal from the flagship, the Chilean flag slid down every yardarm and up went the Stars and Stripes. Soon *Kentucky*, the last ship in line, disappeared over the edge of the world. The visit of the Great White Fleet ended as it had begun, in a wisp of smoke.

The sixteen battleships plowed northward along the South American coast. The seas were calm and the crews were kept busy at drills. On February 19, smoke was sighted on the horizon. Lookouts trained their glasses. The stranger was a man-of-war, and on closer inspection, a cruiser. Her name was the *Bolognesi*. After an exchange of greetings, the newcomer fell into the American formation. The Great White Fleet had entered Peruvian waters. Tomorrow the fleet would make its final port-of-call in South America.

Peru and the United States enjoyed excellent relations, and both nations attached great importance to the fleet's visit to Lima. Every day, Peruvian dailies were filled with accounts of the Great White Fleet, and many Peruvians followed these accounts with avid interest. Of particular note were the stories of the success of the fleet's visit to Brazil. This caused a swelling in national pride that nearly burst the country at the seams. The Peruvians had no intention of being outdone by their Portuguese-speaking neighbors and worked hard to make the fleet's visit to their country the most memorable of the cruise.

On February 20, the Americans found the welcome mat was out. Tens of thousands of wildly cheering

Peruvians had turned out to greet them. People crammed the docks. They lined the shore. Callao's harbor crawled with steamers, fishing barges, sailing craft, and even row-boats. Peruvian and American flags were everywhere. And there was constant rendition of "Viva Los Yankees!" from thousands of throats.

The American ships entered the harbor by squadron. On signal, the battleships redeployed smartly into divisions. The intricacy of the maneuver sent the Peruvians over the top. Peruvian warships in the harbor boomed out thunderous volleys. Small craft chimed in with whistles and bells. While on shore and off, thousands of voices went hoarse adding to the din.

The American ships were ushered to their assigned anchorages. One of the most successful visits of the entire cruise was underway. The first major celebration was hosted by the president himself, Jose Pardo. It was a lavish banquet given in honor of his birthday. By coincidence it was on February 22, the same day as the birthday of America's first president, George Washington. The American fleet was represented at the gala by ten officers and three midshipmen from each command.

The following afternoon, President Pardo made the ten-mile journey from Lima to Callao. He was piped aboard the *Connecticut,* where he paid his respects to the ailing Admiral Evans. While on board, the president made arrangements for the Americans to attend the bullfights in Lima as his personal guests. Some 3,500 officers and ratings were cleared to attend. A pair of trains was chartered for their transportation. From the train station in Lima, some of the enlisted men marched to the stadium, led by a Peruvian military band.

Bullfighting is a spectacle of pomp, ceremony, and tradition. To the *aficionados*, it is a ritual of culture rather than mere competitive sport—a deadly test of honor and courage by man and animal in a duel to the death that inspires its devotees. But none of this mattered to the visiting Yanks. There was not an Ernest Hemingway among them. Most saw the bulls as little more than sacrificial lambs. Many of them were turned off by the carnage. Some openly rooted for the bulls. A number of bluejackets left after only a few fights.

Five colliers arrived in Callao and coaling operations commenced. Refueling was done by division. As a release from the drudgeries of coaling, many bluejackets took in the sights of Lima. The Peruvian capital was one of the most historic cities on the entire cruise. It had been founded by the Spanish conqueror Francisco Pizzaro on January 18, 1535. The fascinating history of Lima can be seen in its historic structures. One such is the *Plaza de Armas* (Main Square), which contains the government house. It was known originally as the House of Pizzaro. Here the conqueror lived and worked until his death in 1541. It later became the official residence of the President of the Republic.

Another is the Lima Cathedral. This Roman Catholic landmark is a major attraction in downtown Lima. The first stone was laid in 1535. Twice damaged by earthquakes, the cathedral has been rebuilt many times. Yet it has stood the test of time for more than four hundred years. It is also the final resting place of Pizzaro the Conqueror.

On the fleet's final day in port, it was customary to reciprocate the hospitality shown by the host with a reception aboard the flagship. In this case, a reception had been planned for President Pardo and his entourage of government functionaries and military officers. But friction developed between Admiral Evans' chief-of-staff and the Minister of the United States in Peru, Leslie Combs. Captain Royal K. Ingersol had taken on many of the duties of command in lieu of the bedridden fleet commander. The dutiful Captain Ingersol suggested to Minister Combs that he invite President Pardo and his entourage for dinner aboard the flagship. Combs refused, deciding that Admiral Thomas, who had been standing in for Admiral Evans at many of the social functions ashore, should deliver the invitation personally. And that the reception should be held aboard Thomas' flagship. Captain Ingersol did not see things this way. He had Admiral Thomas deliver the invitation in Admiral Evans' name. This meant that the reception would not be held on the *Minnesota*, but on the *Connecticut*. With Captain Ingersol in charge of the dinner arrangements, Minister Combs arrived to find his place setting at the far end of the table, beside a Peruvian navy captain. The snub generated the intended response: Combs was deeply offended. However, the dinner went on as planned and was an unqualified success.

The following morning, President Pardo boarded the *Almirante Grau*. The Peruvian cruiser, proudly flying the flag of the commander-in-chief, nosed slowly through the American formation. Aboard the battleships, crews in dress whites and blues manned the railings. In unison, the battleships fired a twenty-one-gun salute to their gracious host. The Peruvian man-of-war cleared the harbor. Just outside the roadstead, the cruiser shut her engines and dropped anchor.

The Great White Fleet lined up astern *Connecticut* and began to exit the harbor.

Each ship took the acknowledgment of President Pardo, with sailors and marines on deck, bands playing the Peruvian National Anthem, and guns booming out salvos. After *Georgia*, the last ship in line, had passed in review, the fleet headed for the open sea. The next leg was 3,100 miles. The destination was Magdalena Bay.

The decision to call on Magdalena Bay was not a popular one in Mexico. Control of the bay had been a bone of contention between Mexico and the United States for much of the nineteenth century. Whalers, seafarers, and other adventurers had been putting into the bay for many years. Other powers besides the United States had also tried to wrest control of the bay from Mexico. Then, in 1864, President Benito Juarez granted a Concession to Jacob Leese to develop an area in Baja that included Magdalena Bay. Terms included the importation of two hundred families to colonize the area in five years. When this and other stipulations were not met, the Concession was turned over to a group of investors known as the Lower California Company. This syndicate indulged in bogus promises to attract settlers, including that of a paradise overflowing with water and trees. This settlement was anything but a paradise, and many who made the trip soon called it quits and returned to the States. This prompted the Mexican Government to evict the American company and take control of the bay.

But Magdalena Bay proved no less attractive to Washington. From the turn of the century till about 1920, ships of the U.S. Navy put into the bay on a regular basis for maneuvers and target practice. This was in clear violation of Mexican sovereignty. This was why when President Diaz agreed to an American concession for five years, the Mexican senate balked. In the end, the U.S. Navy was allowed to maintain a couple of colliers in the bay for the purposes of refueling. But landing parties, gunnery practice toward the shore, and raising the American flag on Mexican soil were forbidden.

The Great White Fleet arrived at Magdalena Bay at 0700 hours on March 12, 1908. Colliers were there waiting with much-needed coal. On hand, too, was a cruiser squadron with targets for gunnery practice. Refueling came first. As each ship replenished its bunkers, it took part in gunnery drills.

Gunnery was the essence of the battleship. The ability to deliver a quick and decisive knockout blow could spell the difference between victory and being destroyed. Gunnery was a source of great pride among the gun crews and led to much-spirited competition. That was why each gunnery officer in the fleet was eager to prove that his crews were the best. But there was more than just proficiency in gunnery that kept a ship in fighting trim. Crews were put through their paces with mine-laying drills, action drills, and range-calibration exercises. In between, marines and sailors went ashore for infantry drills to prepare for the many parades on the West Coast.

It was at Magdalena Bay that the subject of command had reached a critical stage. By this time, Admiral Evans was totally incapacitated. He had been bedridden for much of the voyage and was in constant pain. It was apparent that he could no longer conduct effective command.

Admiral Evans' condition led to a peculiar function of command. Admiral Thomas represented the fleet ashore in all matters of protocol and on board ship with notable guests, diplomats, and other functionaries. Yet the daily routine matters of command were carried out by Captain Ingersol. This prompted Admiral Thomas to observe that he and Admirals Emory and Sperry had to take orders from a captain.

Admiral Evans had in fact been laid up since two days out of Trinidad. When the fleet reached Rio, Evans had a breathing attack so bad it was feared that he might die. But "Fightin' Bob" battled back. He began to show signs of improvement, even to the point of sitting up in bed. Yet a mattress is not a proper command post. So on March 14, Admiral Evans decided to relinquish command.

Rear Admiral Charles M. Thomas was second in command, so he was the nominal choice to replace Admiral Evans. But Thomas was due to retire in October, which was just seven months away. This meant that another change of command would have to be made before the end of the cruise. Thomas had another strike against him as well; he had a bad heart. Admiral Evans saw Admiral Sperry as his replacement. And so he would be. In mid-May, Admiral Sperry would be named commander-in-chief for the cruise from San Francisco to Hampton Roads. But for the time being, Admiral Thomas would hold the reins of command for recognition of his long years of service.

On March 30, *Connecticut* hauled out of Magdalena Bay and barreled north for California. Two days later, the battleship rendezvoused with the *Yankton*. Admiral Evans was transferred to the auxiliary and taken ashore. He was rushed to a hospital in Paso Robles.

Connecticut hurried south to rejoin the fleet at Magdalena Bay. Rear Admiral Charles M. Thomas came aboard and broke out his flag as commander-in-chief. Rear Admiral Sperry assumed the duties as subordinate commander. On April 11, 1908, battleship *Connecticut* led the way out of Magdalena Bay. The Great White Fleet was on its way to San Diego.

CHANGE IN COMMAND

The fleet pushed north, hugging the jagged coastline from Baja all the way to California. Once in U.S. waters, crowds gathered along the shore to catch a glimpse of the ships as they passed. Many cheered them on. Others waved flags. Some even fired guns in the air. These and other outbursts of patriotism followed the fleet all the way to San Diego. On April 14, the fleet dropped anchor off Coronado.

An armada of small craft besieged the task force. Many came right up alongside to bombard the battleships with flowers. And there were oranges, too, thousands of them. In fact, more than thirty thousand oranges found their way into the galleys of the Great White Fleet. Officers granted liberty were overwhelmed by the reception ashore. A seven hundred-foot pier had been built to accommodate the fleet's landing parties. The first group of officers who came ashore never made it off the pier. They were scooped up and carried off by a horde of delirious merrymakers who had been waiting for them. That night the city was ablaze with lights, and huge bonfires burned along the beaches.

The next morning, a brigade-sized landing party of sailors and marines came ashore. The men marched through the cheering crowds to City Park for an official welcome. After the official greeting came tours of the city and the surrounding countryside. For the young sailors and marines, many of whom were a long way from home, the outpouring of friendship by the people of San Diego would not soon be forgotten. For the officers, the highlight of the San Diego stop was a dinner and ball held at the Hotel Del Coronado on April 17. The fact that it was Good Friday made it awkward for some of the more religiously inclined. But it was a standing order for the officers to attend, and attend they did.

At 0600 hours the next day, the fleet headed north to Los Angeles. It was only a ten-hour steam. But just like the cruise to San Diego, crowds jammed the water's edge to catch a glimpse of the passing battleships. When the fleet arrived off San Pedro, thousands were on the beaches waiting for the crews to come ashore. But the official welcome was not until the following day. So the fleet anchored in the harbor for the night.

The next day was April 19, Easter Sunday. The fleet broke into divisions. First Division remained in San Pedro. Second Division moved on to Long Beach. Third Division went to Santa Monica and Fourth Division to Redondo Beach. That night, Los Angeles was treated to a searchlight show that dazzled the crowds. The city showed its appreciation by opening itself up to the enlisted men for a four-day holiday. On the 23rd, two hundred and fifty officers were taken on a tour of Los Angeles, including Hollywood and Pasadena. At Sawtelle, thousands of Civil War veterans lined the route in salute. At Santa Monica, practically the entire town turned out to show its gratitude. The next day, it was the turn of the enlisted men. Three thousand of them got the red carpet treatment, just like the officers the day before.

On April 25, the fleet reassembled for the short hop to Santa Barbara. An announcement was made that prior to the fleet's departure it would put on a show with maneuvers. All that day and night, an army of onlookers invaded Santa Monica for the show. Hotels and motels quickly ran out of rooms. People slept on the beaches, rooftops, or wherever else they could find space. The next morning, to the disappointment of the crowd, a heavy fog blanketed the harbor and the maneuvers were cut short.

The battleships left Los Angeles and groped their way through the murk toward Santa Barbara. About midday, the fog lifted and the fleet arrived several hours later. The visit began with a reception for the officers at the residence of retired Admiral Bowman McCalla. More banquets and balls for the officers were held at the stylish Potter Hotel. But the city did precious little for the enlisted men. In fact, the city's treatment of the ratings was downright shameful. Sky-high rates for accommodations not only placed a great hardship on the sailors, but also for their families coming to meet them. Peculation was rampant, too, with food, drink, and entertainment. At one eatery, rock-wielding bluejackets smashed windows and broke tables and chairs. Many sailors took trains back to Los Angeles, where they found the welcome mat out waiting for them.

On April 30, the fleet left for Monterey. On May 2, First Squadron pushed on for Santa Cruz. Two days later, Second Squadron joined up with First Squadron. Later that same day, the torpedo-boat flotilla arrived. While up north, the Pacific Fleet Cruiser Squadron, which left Seattle on May 1, arrived at San Francisco to await the Great White Fleet.

Early the next day, *Connecticut* doubled back to Monterey. Rear Admiral Evans, who had taken a train up from Paso Robles, was piped aboard. He was still in great pain, but nothing was going to keep the intrepid commander from manning the bridge of his flagship. Robley D. Evans was going to lead his fleet in its triumphal entry into San Francisco.

From the earliest stages of planning, San Francisco was considered the highlight port-of-call on the West Coast. The city was still digging out from the earthquake that had devastated it eighteen months before. But the people came together. They rebuilt their shattered neighborhoods and dug deep into their pockets for the money to bring the fleet to their city. In fact, most of the money raised for the fleet's visit had come from private donations, some $75,000.

Five days before the fleet arrived, more than half a million people descended on San Francisco. They came streaming into the city by any means they could: by railroad, carriage, automobile, bicycle, and even shoe leather. Soon the most popular sign in the Bay City was "No Vacancy." Just like at Santa Monica, people slept on rooftops, beaches, and hillsides. Wherever there was a space, there was as a body.

Battleships *Nebraska* and *Wisconsin* arrived, joining the other battlewagons of the Great White Fleet. The Pacific Fleet's Cruiser Squadron, the torpedo-boat flotilla, and the auxiliaries attached to the round-the-world cruise all massed off San Francisco Bay. A total of forty-two warships and auxiliaries, the largest concentration of naval might ever gathered in the Western Hemisphere to date. And it would all be led by "Fightin' Bob Evans."

The fleet spent the night of May 5 anchored off the Bay. In the morning, a bright sun burned away the darkness and shed light upon the greatest migration of humanity ever gathered on the West Coast. Upwards of a million people lined the Golden Gate. Up on Telegraph Hill, white letters standing fifty feet high spelled *Welcome*. Small craft were thicker than locust on the waters of the Golden Gate. But this armada of lightweights gave way to the approaching concentration of big guns and armor plate. Forty-two vessels, steaming in a circle two miles wide, advanced resolutely into the Bay. Army forts standing sentinel fired their batteries in salute. The fleet, with *Connecticut* at its head, steamed past Angel Island, then the Pacific Fleet anchorage. As the fleet came upon the gunboat *Yorktown*, *Connecticut* loosed a seventeen-gun salute to the flag of the Secretary of the Navy.

The entire fleet anchored in San Francisco Bay. All flag officers and battleship skippers were shuttled over to *Connecticut* to pay their respects to Admiral Evans' two-star flag. Following this formality, Admiral Evans was to accompany Secretary of the Navy Metcalf in a review of the fleet, after which he was to take part in a ceremony that was to affect the official change in command. But the day's activities had proven to be too much for him. He was whisked away to the St. Francis Hotel for a much-needed rest.

The next day, May 7, was the day of the grand parade. Companies of sailors and marines from both the Atlantic and Pacific Fleets were put ashore. They numbered more than 7,500. It was at that time that the largest U.S. naval force ever landed in peacetime or in war. They were joined by army regulars, California National Guardsmen, State

Police, veterans groups, and a host of organizations too numerous to mention. Admiral Evans shared a carriage with the mayor of San Francisco. The resolute commander braved much pain to acknowledge the tens of thousands who lined the parade route, all cheering for "Fightin' Bob Evans" and his fleet.

On May 8, Secretary of the Navy Metcalf boarded the *Yorktown*. Beneath the clear blue California sky, hundreds of thousands watched and cheered as the secretary reviewed the fleet. *Yorktown* sailed first by the armored cruisers of the Pacific Fleet. The gunboat then came about and made for the battleships. First Battleship Squadron was reviewed, followed by Second Battleship Squadron. Last came the tin cans of the torpedo-boat flotilla. Aboard each ship, officers, ratings, and marines in dress whites and blues stood stiffly on parade, with flags and pennants flying and bands playing proudly to the delight of the crowds ashore.

That evening, the City of San Francisco hosted a grand reception at the St. Francis Hotel. The gala was every bit as much a testimonial for Admiral Evans as it was a celebration for the Great White Fleet. From his wheelchair, Admiral Evans gave his farewell address. It was his last public appearance as a flag officer. Following his address, Admiral Evans was wheeled to his room. The next day, May 9, "Fightin' Bob Evans" and his family were on a train headed for Washington, D.C., and retirement. His naval career, which began during the Civil War, was over. Rear Admiral Charles M. Thomas officially assumed command of the Great White Fleet, but this honorary posting was temporary, only six days. Thomas, too, was slated for retirement. However, Thomas' departure was of tragically short duration. His weak heart gave out and he died on July 3, 1908, in Del Monte, California. On May 15, Rear Admiral Charles Stillman Sperry was named third and final commander of the Great White Fleet.

Charles Stillman Sperry was born on September 3, 1847, in Brooklyn, New York. He entered the Naval Academy in 1862, at the time the youngest cadet ever to do so. He graduated in 1866, near the top of his class. He was highly regarded for his intelligence and academic interest. His peers considered him a better-than-average tactician. And his reputation as a "spit and polish" officer became well-known throughout the fleet.

Sperry commanded the *Yorktown* in November 1898. He later served as a senior officer in the South Squadron of the Asiatic Fleet. He twice taught mathematics at the Naval Academy and later assumed the position of President of the Naval War College for three years.

Following his promotion to flag rank, he was assigned to the United States' delegation to the Geneva Convention, and later to the Second Hague Convention in 1907. Sperry's claim to fame is as commander-in-chief of the Great White Fleet from its departure at San Francisco to its return to Hampton Roads on February 22, 1909. Sperry retired from the Service on September 3, 1909. His retirement was short-lived, as he was returned to duty. This posting, too, was of short duration. Admiral Sperry died in Washington D.C. on February 1, 1911.

It was while the fleet was at Magdalena Bay that Washington officially announced the route of return. From San Francisco Bay, the fleet would cross the Pacific

Ocean to the Indian Ocean, on to the Mediterranean via the Suez Canal, and then across the Atlantic for Hampton Roads and home. The release of the itinerary was immediately followed by a flood of invitations from nations along the projected route. However, the "official" announcement of the fleet's route of return merely confirmed what Washington had planned all along. All this was borne out by the invitations accepted from a number of nations before the fleet ever arrived at Magdalena Bay.

One of the first nations to request a visit was Australia. The nation's overture was expressed in a letter from Prime Minister Alfred Deakin to John P. Bray, American Consul-General in Melbourne. The prime minister also wrote to Whitelow Reid, American ambassador to the Court of St. James. Both letters were forwarded to Secretary of State Elihu Root. The secretary urged the president to accept the gracious invitation and for obvious strategic reasons. The Pacific Rim was becoming an important arena on the world stage. It was in the best interest of the United States to foster relationships with nations such as Australia and New Zealand. Besides a common language, these were nations with which the United States shared ethnic, cultural, religious, and political similarities. Australia, too, recognized the potential of such a partnership. Like the United States, Japanese immigration was a major concern in Australia. But of greater concern was the threat posed by growing Japanese power. While it was true that Britain and Japan were allies, the pullback of the Royal Navy was a major cause of unease in Canberra. Not only would Australia have to embark on a naval construction program of her own, but it was necessary to open a relationship with the one Caucasian, Christian power that was close enough and strong enough to offset the threat from up north. That power was the United States.

Though in favor of the fleet's visit to Australia from the start, Root thought that the public release of Deakin's letter to Bray was unwise. Root did not want to offend the British Foreign Office with any premature announcements. At the president's cabinet meeting on February 21, 1908, Root was overruled. Secretary of the Navy Metcalf released the correspondence as well as other diplomatic communications.

The release of Deakin's letter did not set well in London. Many, like Parliamentary Undersecretary Winston Churchill, were against the visit. But publication of the letter forced Britain's hand. The admiralty, with many of its ships tied up in the North Sea facing off against the German fleet, was in no position to offer much in the way of resistance. This left the Foreign Office with no other recourse but to sanction the visit.

New Zealand, not wanting to be left out in the cold, moved quickly. Prime Minister Joseph Ward petitioned the American Consul-General, William A. Prickett, on March 4. Prickett, ignorant of the Australian situation, thought the issue of the fleet's visit to his post hardly important enough to justify an immediate request to Washington. So he forwarded Ward's proposal by common mail. However, when the Australia visit was made public, Prickett cabled Washington right away. On March 16, Prime Minister Ward petitioned the British Governor Lord Plunkett to issue an official invitation. With the Australian stop a foregone conclusion, the Great White Fleet's visit to Auckland was assured.

Two days later, on March 18, Japan's Ambassador to

the United States Baron Kagoro Takahira delivered the Imperial Government's official invitation. The Japanese were well aware of the growing success of the Great White Fleet and the opportunity a visit by the fleet would provide for improving relations with Washington. President Roosevelt accepted Tokyo's solicitation.

In drawing up the itinerary for the Pacific leg of the cruise, it was necessary to reconcile the navy's refueling needs and the scheduled fall target practice in Manila with the State Department's political agenda and competing invitations. Stops planned for the Dutch East Indies, Canada, Britain and a half a hundred other places were just not possible to fit in. Britain, however, did make the port facilities of Malta and Gibraltar available for the fleet when it reached the Mediterranean.

One source of controversy was left off the original itinerary: China. That is until March 23, when China's ambassador, Wu Ting-fang, delivered an invitation from China's Ministry of Foreign Affairs. The next day, President Roosevelt and his cabinet met to decide on a course of action. In dealing with China, they were forced to tread a minefield of political intricacies and pitfalls. When a consensus could not be reached, advice was sought from the American Minister to China, William W. Rockhill. Rockhill urged caution. He warned that Peking might try to use the fleet's visit to implicate Washington in a Chinese attempt to overturn the rights of Japan and the European powers. He cautioned that any port chosen for the visit must not be a bottleneck that left the battleships susceptible to a surprise Japanese attack. The great urban centers like Shanghai were to be avoided as well, because the potential for civil agitation was too great. Instead

Rockhill suggested that the fleet call on Amoy. Amoy was isolated from the great cities and offered a protected anchorage. Roosevelt and his cabinet agreed. China was added to the itinerary.

The issue of China demonstrated the State Department's growing influence in planning the fleet's itinerary. From Hampton Roads to San Francisco, the cruise had been the show of the White House and the Navy Department. But by Magdalena Bay it was becoming clear that the Atlantic Fleet Battleship Force was not anything like the Russian Baltic Fleet of 1904–05. Both man and machine were proving themselves capable of defending America's interests. This instilled growing confidence in the White House of the fleet's ability to project power thousands of miles from America's shores. At the same time, the State Department was finding that in the officers and men of the fleet they had able globetrotting ambassadors who were successfully selling America abroad. For the Navy Department it was a marvelous public relations coup, and one that would sell to the public and to Congress the fleet's ability to handle its role as America's first line of defense.

On May 18, *Connecticut* led the Great White Fleet out of San Francisco Bay. The fleet was on its way to call on the ports of the Pacific Northwest. The battleships hugged the coast so that the excited throngs that had gathered along the way could see them.

On May 21, the fleet transited the Juan de Fuca Strait and entered Puget Sound. A half a million people awaited the fleet in Seattle. They had streamed in from

Washington, Oregon, Idaho, Montana, and even British Columbia. Celebrations and festivities filled the next two days, capped off by a huge parade.

Each ship was presented with a mascot, a bear cub. As if the crews did not have enough mascots already. Monkeys, goats, pigs, parrots, and other species, had all been collected while the fleet rounded the South American continent. This leap into wild kingdom would be given a real shot in the arm when the fleet called on places like New Zealand, Australia, and the Philippines.

The fleet dispersed upon leaving Seattle. First and Third Divisions returned to San Francisco. Second Division went on to Bremerton, while Fourth Division visited Tacoma. At San Francisco, *Connecticut* went into Hunter's Point Navy Yard for a much-needed refit. One by one, her sisters followed suit, as the fleet was made ready for the Pacific cruise. There was also a change in the batting order. *Maine* and *Alabama* were scratched from the roster. The former because of an unquenchable appetite for coal and the latter because of a cracked cylinder head. Their places were taken by *Nebraska*, fresh from her shakedown cruise, and *Wisconsin*, fresh from a refit.

Rear Admiral Charles Stillman Sperry was ready to take his place as commander-in-chief of the Great White Fleet. He was also commander of First Battleship Squadron and First Battleship Division. Second in command was Rear Admiral William H. Emory. He also commanded Second Battleship Squadron and Third Battleship Division. Captain Richard Wainwright of *Louisiana* was promoted to rear admiral. He flew his flag aboard *Georgia* as commander of Second Battleship Division. Also promoted to flag rank was Captain Seaton Schroeder of *Virginia*. He unfurled his new two-star flag aboard *Wisconsin* as commander of Fourth Battleship Division.

On June 25, it was announced that the fleet would return home to Hampton Roads on February 22, 1909, on George Washington's birthday. With its command structure in place and the date of arrival fixed, the Great White Fleet was ready to depart San Francisco. Next stop was Hawaii, the first port-of-call on the Pacific leg of the epic round-the-world cruise.

DOWN UNDER

The fleet was scheduled to leave San Francisco on July 7. Unlike the fleet's arrival, there was no fanfare attached to its departure. Nevertheless, thousands turned out to see the ships off. But not everybody in the task force it seemed was eager to leave. Earlier in the day, one hundred and twenty-nine sailors had failed to answer the morning muster. A search revealed that none of the absentees were hurt or sick. That meant only one thing: They were AWOL. With the fleet due to leave at two that afternoon, there was little chance of rounding up more than just a few of the deserters. So rather than upset the timetable, the stragglers were left behind.

At 1400 hours, *Connecticut* began to make her way out of the Bay. One by one, the other battlewagons fell astern the flagship. That is, all of them except *Nebraska*. A number of her crew had taken sick with scarlet fever. The ship was immediately put under quarantine. The afflicted were removed and the entire ship was fumigated. On July 9, *Nebraska* was given a clean bill of health. The battleship got up steam and quickly put to sea. She overhauled the fleet five days later. By that time, the Great White Fleet was just two days out of Hawaii.

Early on the morning of July 16, lookouts spotted the Hawaiian Islands. But instead of heading straight for Oahu, Admiral Sperry ordered a detour. He headed for Malokai first. The island was home to a colony of lepers.

These social outcasts rarely had contact with or sympathy from the outside world, but now the navy was about to give them a real lift. Sperry positioned his fleet four miles off shore so as to provide the exiles a panoramic view. The sufferers came streaming out of their houses, waving and cheering as the battlewagons slid majestically by. Brother Joseph Dutton would later write to Admiral Sperry, "Those sixteen battleships that have the full confidence of America came down the lane with a friendly nod and passed on, so dignified and beautiful, this July morning... It makes us better Americans and may God bless everyone who has even a little to do with bringing about this great pleasure. In all this I am speaking for the people of the leper settlement."[1]

Following this gesture of goodwill, the fleet headed for Honolulu. In 1908, Honolulu was not a major port. The harbor was small and the facilities were not up to accommodating an entire fleet. Only First Division was allowed to enter the harbor. The rest of the fleet, except for Third Division, anchored just outside. Third Division continued on to Lahaina to coal.

At the time of the arrival of the Great White Fleet, Hawaii was not the popular romantic getaway it was later to become. Many still referred to them as the Sandwich Islands. Despite the fact it was American territory, many Americans still had not heard of the place.

The Hawaiian Islands were first settled by the Polynesians around 500 AD. They were followed some five hundred years later by the Tahitians. The Tahitians eventually went on to establish the dominant position. All this changed in 1778, when the British explorer James Cook found the islands. He named the future paradise the Sandwich Islands after the First Lord of the Admiralty, John Montagu, also known as the Fourth Earl of Sandwich.

In the beginning, Cook was seen as a god by some of the Hawaiians. Many even thought him to be the legendary Lono, the deity of peace and fertility. According to Hawaiian mythology, Lono was supposed to descend to the earth on a rainbow. Cook's arrival by sailing ship was much more mundane, and it was not long before the natives began to lose their faith. This loss of faith eventually turned to distrust, and in a later fracas at Kealakekau Bay, James Cook was clubbed and stabbed to death.

One of those who witnessed Cook's murder was a ferocious warrior named Kamehameha. King Kamehameha, as he was later known, unified the Hawaiian Islands and established a monarchy. But by the early 1800s, his hold on power was being undermined by the growing presence of the white man. Kamehameha decided to adopt the ways of the foreigner. He joined with the Americans in a lucrative trade involving the islands' sandalwood forests. But no amount of complicity could halt the growing domination of the Americans. Their whaling ships called on the islands in such growing numbers that Hawaii became the hub to the Pacific whaling industry. Big money followed the whalers, and much of this money went into developing the sugar industry.

But by the mid-1800s, the native population was in decline. This meant that other sources of cheap labor had to be found to work the sugar plantations. The answer was immigration. They came to the islands in droves from China, Japan, Puerto Rico, Korea, the Philippines, and even Portugal. With the growing power of the sugar interests, the Yankee grip on the islands tightened. In 1868, the United States grabbed Midway Island to the north.

The navy eventually became the arbiter of American affairs in Hawaii. In 1887, the navy obtained exclusive rights to erect repair facilities and a coaling station at Pearl Harbor. This boosted the fortunes of the sugar barons. For now they could peddle their product on the mainland duty free.

Then, in 1898, the Spanish-American War changed the strategic dynamics of the Pacific Rim. The American victory saw the United States replace Spain as a major colonial power in the East. Overnight Hawaii took on a whole new strategic significance. In response, Washington decided to annex the islands. This allowed the navy to expand its presence. Work began on developing Pearl Harbor. In 1908, the harbor was dredged and a shipyard was built. By the time Sperry's fleet arrived, the American hegemony of Hawaii was firmly established.

The beaches were jammed with those waiting for the sailors to come ashore. Out in the harbor, small craft of all types swarmed the battleships. Yachts, sailboats, outrigger canoes. Many were colorfully adorned. All were full of people eager to take part in this once-in-a-lifetime event. The first order of business was for Admiral Sperry to call on Governor Frear. His barge was lowered over the side. When the admiral was safely aboard, the helmsman started for the beach. He gingerly picked his way through the traffic jam and got his commander ashore. Sperry paid his respects to the governor and then returned to his flagship. The governor returned the favor later in the day with a visit aboard *Connecticut*.

The following day, *Connecticut* played host to a number of foreign dignitaries. Coming to call were diplomats from England, Peru, Mexico, Norway, Sweden, Germany, Portugal, France, Japan, and China. At the same time ashore, sailors and marines marched through the streets of Honolulu. There were flowers everywhere, carnations, roses, and leis. Sometimes girls would dart out on to the parade route, lasso a sailor with a necklace of flowers, and follow it up with a smother of kisses.

Over the next five days, ships entered the harbor singly to coal. Those crew members not assigned to coaling detail were able to go ashore. Bluejackets were treated like royalty, taking in the beaches, luaus, and parades. On July 16, the festive atmosphere was marred by an accident aboard *Kearsarge*. A steam pipe burst, scalding several sailors and starting a fire. The blaze was quickly extinguished. Damage was minor and repairs were made in short order. The injured sailors were treated and returned to duty. The mishap aboard *Kearsarge* did not delay the fleet's scheduled departure. At 1800 hours on July 22, *Connecticut* led the fleet out of Honolulu. One ship was left behind, *Minnesota*. The Third Division flagship was detached to collect the mail. She would have to catch up to the fleet on the way to the next stop, New Zealand.

The steam from Honolulu to Auckland was 3,850 miles. This was the longest stretch of ocean on the entire cruise. However, such distances were no longer a concern for the Great White Fleet. Much had been learned in the areas of fuel efficiency and cruise control while rounding the South American continent. Through trial and error, the fleet's engineers had become quite skilled at monitoring their fuel supplies. They learned how to get the most miles out of every ton of coal that was burned. Fuel conservation was a particularly vital concern for the short-legged ships. But the fleet's engineers had learned to ply their trade so well that not one ship coasted into any port with empty bunkers during the entire cruise.

Minnesota caught up to the fleet on July 28. A halt was called and the mail was parceled out to the task force. Homesick sailors took time for the Dear John round up, but the pause was a short one. The fleet was soon on the move again. Four days later, it reached Samoa.

Samoa was not a scheduled stop. The fleet was to conduct a brief sail-by and then continue on its way. *Connecticut* led the parade past Tutuila. The battleships rounded the eastern tip of the island and then traced its southern shore. They breezed by Pago Pago. In the harbor was the navy station ship *Annapolis,* which fired a volley in salute.

Then, like a giant snake, Sperry's line of ships wound its way round the island and out into the open sea.

On August 7, the fleet plowed straight into a storm. High winds and lofty seas tossed the ships about. For the next twenty-four hours, they endured nature's wrath. But soon the tempest subsided and the skies cleared. Calls went out from the flagship for damage control assessments. None of the ships reported major damage and none of the men were lost. With his fleet intact, Sperry continued on a southwesterly course, doing a healthy twelve knots across flat seas. Auckland, the next port-of-call, was only twenty-four hours away.

At 0710, on Sunday morning, August 9, the American warships began to appear through a curtain of mist. A lookout on board NZS *Amokura* spotted them and raised the alarm. The maritime training ship fired a thirteen-gun salute. Upwards of 100,000 noisy New Zealanders had lined Waitemata Harbor and Rangitoto Channel to welcome the globetrotters. Sperry thrilled the huge audience by having his ships cut a huge S into the glass-like channel with exquisite precision.

A swarm of small boats intercepted the fleet as it rounded North Head. The armada crossed the channel and entered Waitemata Harbor. The battleships picked their way through the maze of small craft to their anchorage, and there they were berthed.

The previous evening, Prime Minister Ward had arrived by train from Wellington. He was accompanied by most of his cabinet, as well as many of the members of Parliament. With many of its elected officials unavailable, the Government of New Zealand had no other recourse but to shut down for the next five days.

Official greetings were exchanged by Admiral Sperry and Prime Minister Ward. The popular welcome was scheduled for the following day. That morning, Admiral Sperry, at the head of a large entourage of officers and ratings, came ashore. At the landing ceremonies, twenty thousand New Zealanders were waiting. The ceremonies opened with speeches trumpeting the common language and heritage shared by the two nations. This was followed by a reception for Admiral Sperry and his officers hosted by local officials. Then it was on to Albert Park for the Ceremony of Friendship. Sixteen oak seedlings, each representing a vessel of the Great White Fleet, were planted. That afternoon, some fifty thousand people took in a parade featuring American sailors and marines and military personnel from New Zealand. A state banquet crowned the day's activities.

Organizations like the YMCA opened their doors to the visiting Americans. Many a lonely Yank wondered in and found an oasis of smiling faces and coffee pots going twenty-four hours a day. Carriages and trams worked overtime, as sailors and marines took in the sights. And, of course, Americans opened their wallets in Auckland, buying gifts and tokens of their visit to send to loved ones back home. Yet for servicemen a long way from home, nothing replaced the mail as a way of keeping in touch with family and friends. And from New Zealand, American sailors and marines sent forty-thousand post-cards back to the States.

On August 11, members of the New Zealand Parliament and their families were piped aboard *Connecticut* for a reception. Prime Minister Ward recip-rocated by inviting many of the American officers to the Ellerslie Race Track. This was followed the next day by a train ride north to a resort at Rotorua to bask in the ther-mal springs. That evening, the final night in port, thou-sands of New Zealanders mobbed the wharves to see the Americans off. Many were sorry to see them go. Many of the Americans were sorry to leave and would fondly remember the down-home friendship and hospitality of these English-speaking white people with whom they had so much in common.

The next day, August 14, Prime Minister Ward boarded

a government steamer to review the American warships. The steamer circled the harbor once, then proceeded out into the channel for the review. The battleships got up steam. *Connecticut* assumed her rightful position at the head of the column. The Constitution State Battleship exited the harbor and passed in review. One by one, her sisters followed suit. On the quarter deck of each warship, the ship's band played the national anthem of each nation. As *Kentucky,* the last ship in line, passed in review, Prime Minister Ward led his entourage in three rousing cheers for the United States.

The Great White Fleet rounded New Zealand's North Cape and issued into the Tasman Sea. The crossing to Australia would not be an easy one. For the second time in two weeks, the task force had to face the ire of Mother Nature. The storm struck on August 18. Ships became gripped in a maelstrom of stirring gales and towering seas. Giant rollers of water carried ships upwards, almost into the sky, then sent them rocketing down watery slopes into troughs of frothy violence. For two days, the angry Tasman Sea manhandled the ships of the Great White Fleet. Then suddenly a bright sun appeared. It burned away the hooded skies, stilled the winds, and calmed the seas. Again the flagship put out the call. And again the fleet's luck had held. No men were reported lost and damage was negligible. Officers busied their men with cleaning the ships and getting them ready for the next port-of-call. In twenty-four hours, they would sail into one of the most memorable liberty ports on the entire cruise, Sydney.

Ashore the Australians were champing at the bit. More

than half a million of them were camped out, men, women, and children. The encampment stretched for almost fifteen miles, from Manly to North Head, and from Botany Bay to South Head. Some had been up the entire night keeping watch. Their vigil ended at 5:00 a.m.

From out to sea, lights burned slowly through the fading darkness. Mastheads poked up from the horizon. One by one, vague silhouettes took shape until sixteen battleships came into focus, plowing resolutely on in a single column as they closed the coastline. By 9:00 a.m., Sperry's task force was off Botany Bay. In no time, the fleet became ringed in by an armada of small craft. Inside the encirclement, Sperry maneuvered his men-of-war into a huge square and made for Sydney Harbor. As *Connecticut* passed North Head, it loosed a twenty-one-gun salute to Fort Denison. The garrison inside the bastion replied in kind.

The fleet split up into divisions. Each ship, in turn, was coaxed into a prearranged anchorage. Ashore, bands and orchestras played the "Star-Spangled Banner" and other American patriotic songs.

The Australians had planned for this visit for a long time, and Sydney had no intention of being outdone by any other city. A plethora of activities had been planned—banquets and balls, galas and games, teas and tours. Americans and Australians competed against one another in such sports as boomerang throwing, buck jumping, wood chopping, rifle matches, boxing, and baseball. Yet despite the superb planning, the Australians ran into a legal snag.

Among the scheduled activities were the parades. This meant, of course, that American sailors and marines were going to have to march. But according to Imperial Regulations, armed parties were forbidden to land on Australian soil. Admiral Sperry pointed out respectfully that his men would not march without their arms. So a compromise was reached: The American crews could retain their arms, but their ammunition would remain aboard their ships.

The following day, August 21, a naval brigade landed at Farm Cove at Woolloomooloo Bay. From here, the Yanks marched into Sydney. One of the streets, Pitt Street, had been renamed "American Avenue." Sailors and marines marched down the road to a never-ending chorus of applause and cheers. The bluejackets and leathernecks marched to the Domain where they received the city's official welcome. Then they did an about-face and trekked across the city to Mrs. Macquarie's Point for a huge luncheon.

A number of trains had been set aside for the sailors and marines so they could see the sights, courtesy of the New South Wales Government. The Americans were astonished at the size of the crowds that came out to greet them. Sometimes entire towns turned out. One such was Newcastle, just north of Sydney, where the Yanks were treated as conquering heroes. The mayor, city council, an honor guard, two brass bands, and hundreds of people besieged the railroad station.

The highpoint of the Sydney visit occurred on August 23. The site was Centennial Park. United States sailors and marines were joined by Royal Navy and Commonwealth naval and military personnel from New South Wales for an official review. There were twelve thousand in all, the largest military review ever held in Australia up to that time. As they marched, more than a quarter million people cheered them on. It was one of the most memorable events in the history of Sydney.

August 26 was the last full day in Sydney. And a full day it was, featuring more rifle matches, baseball games, and garden parties. At the Sydney Cricket Grounds, nearly ten thousand school children put on an extravaganza for the visitors. The curtain came down that evening with a lavish dinner held aboard *Connecticut*.

At 0800 hours on the following morning, the battleships got up steam and upped anchor. Tens of thousands turned out to see the fleet off. They watched as the task force slid lazily out of the harbor. Sailors and marines manned the railings, watching the city recede from view. Years later, many of them would fondly recall the friendship and kindness shown to them by the people of Sydney. Likewise, they would never forget the goodwill of their next port-of-call. Two nights and six hundred miles later, the task force was outside Melbourne.

At 1100 hours on August 29, the fleet skirted Port Philip Head and began the thirty-mile run to Hobson's Bay. Just like at Auckland and Sydney, the task force became besieged by a fleet of small craft and steamers. The battleships managed to slalom their way through traffic and entered their anchorage in Hobson's Bay. By the time the ships were berthed, it was three in the afternoon; too late for any activities except for those of an official nature between the officers of the squadron and government representatives ashore. The next day was Sunday, and St. Patrick's Cathedral opened its doors to the visitors. Over one thousand American sailors attended a mass celebrated in their honor. They were among the 2,500 bluejackets who were granted liberty on the first day.

The official welcome was on Monday. Banquets, games, and theater performances were among the activities planned for the visitors. That night, many American sailors joined in on the huge torchlight parade that wound its way through the city.

Unlike in Sydney, American sailors and marines enjoyed more free time in Melbourne. Many Yanks wondered in and out of stores, took in the sights, or found the girls. Appealing in his uniform and with his pockets bulging with Yankee Greenbacks, the American sailor had no trouble picking up girls. It was not unusual to find a sailor or marine with a girl on each arm. Such was the time the Yanks were having on the streets that a dinner planned for three thousand enlisted personnel barely drew a handful.

The only real gripe about Melbourne was getting into the city. From Hobson's Bay, where the American fleet was anchored, it was a thirty-minute shuttle by launch to Williamstown. From here, it was a hike to the railroad station, where it was another forty-minute train ride to Melbourne. But this inconvenience melted in the face of the warm welcome shown by the people of this great city. In fact, Melbourne would go down as the favorite port-of-call. This can be seen in the number of deserters. In Auckland, only one failed to return to his ship at the time of sailing. Sydney saw less than twenty unaccounted for. But at Melbourne, over two hundred went missing. Many were later rounded up. But in the end, more than a hundred men went AWOL in Melbourne.

Thursday was made an official holiday in Melbourne. With much of the city closed down, thousands gathered for the military review and parade. But the stars of the day were not the Americans, but the young naval cadets of Ballarat. These intrepid young men, ranging in ages from eleven to sixteen, eschewed public transportation and marched to Melbourne. Tired and footsore, these proud lads trudged eighty miles in five days. These sailors-in-the-making captured the hearts and minds of the American bluejackets. Many of the lads were actually carried in the parade by jubilant Yanks.

Fleet week ended with a giant fireworks extravaganza at Albert Park. Liberty was officially over at 2300 hours. The scene at the railroad station was right out of a movie, with young ladies hugging and kissing departing sailors and marines. Girls snagged hats, buttons, and other mementos that could be had. Many would miss their Yankee lovers.

On Sunday morning, September 6, the entire fleet, save *Kansas*, slipped out of Hobson's Bay and out into the open sea. The task force sliced across the Great Australian Bight. The Bight is a body of water known for its powerful rollers. Yet despite the heavy seas, the 1,300-mile crossing proved uneventful. Five days later, on September 11, the Great White Fleet reached Albany.

Connecticut fired a twenty-one-gun salute to the fort guarding the harbor entrance. The bastion returned the gesture. Already in the harbor lay the British cruiser HMS *Gibraltar* and the Chilean training ship *General Baquedano*. Both vessels rendered gun salutes to the flag of Admiral Sperry. Governor of West Australia, Rear Admiral F.G.D. Bedford, exchanged official greetings with Admiral Sperry.

Albany lies on the southwestern tip of Australia.

Hardly a metropolis, this proud community gave way nothing to Sydney and Melbourne in its efforts to welcome the fleet. A number of festivities had been planned for the visiting Americans. However, the main reason for the stopover was to coal. For the next stop was Manila, some 3,500 miles away.

Coal was a nagging problem for Admiral Sperry while visiting the Land Down Under. Six colliers had been expected to rendezvous with the fleet at Albany. Only three were there waiting when the battleships arrived. The same thing happened in New Zealand. Six colliers carrying American coal had been contracted to meet the fleet at Auckland. Again only three showed up. This left Sperry's task force short more than sixteen thousand tons. Thus the scramble was on for more coal.

No provisions had been made for refueling in either Sydney or Melbourne. This is because there was supposed to have been enough coal waiting for the fleet at Auckland to fuel the run to Albany. To Commander Albert W. Grant, chief-of-staff to Admiral Sperry, fell the unenviable task of scraping together the needed supplies of coal. He opened negotiations with local coal company officials. Next he had to take on the local labor unions, but the resourceful Grant managed to secure the necessary supplies of fuel. Over six thousand tons was made available by rerouting colliers and pinching supplies from other vessels. While in Melbourne, a rerouted collier met the fleet with five thousand tons. This was augmented by an additional two thousand tons purchased from local stock.

However, the shortage of coal at Albany threatened to

upset Sperry's schedule. Refueling operations were conducted from the trio of colliers that had made it to the rendezvous. Then, on September 15, two of the delinquent colliers arrived. Bad weather was to blame for the pair's tardiness. But the third missing collier was still en route and not expected for another two weeks. Sperry could not wait that long. He would make do with what he had. He ordered another round of refueling.

The disruption of his coal supplies infuriated Admiral Sperry. He blamed Admiral Cowles, Chief of the Bureau of Equipment, for the debacle. But Cowles could not be expected to shoulder all the blame. The last-minute announcement of the Pacific leg of the cruise made the shipping of American coal to a smattering of ports round the globe a tough proposition. Pricing had to be negotiated with the companies involved. Shipping schedules had to be drawn up. Colliers had to be loaded and then routed. Yet the problem lay not with shipping schedules, competitive pricing, or bad weather. The simple fact was that the United States Navy did not have enough colliers. Again this meant that the navy's long-range operations were not possible without the support of foreign-flagged carriers.

Always lurking in the back of Sperry's mind was the hard reality that the Great White Fleet had to rely on the British merchant marine for its fuel. He knew that in the Russo-Japanese War of 1904–05, Britain stood by its ally and refused to supply the czar's navy with coal. So this prompted the great question: If the Great White Fleet came to blows with the Imperial Navy, would London fulfill its treaty obligations and stand by Tokyo? Or would the British continue to supply the coal in an effort to court

American assistance in the face of the growing German threat?

RAPPROCHEMENT

Kansas arrived at Albany in September 15, the same day as the delinquent colliers. Aboard the battleship were 458 bags of mail. Also aboard were more than a hundred deserters from Melbourne. This left more than one hundred strays still at large. However, with a schedule to keep, the stragglers were written off.

Three days later, the fleet was ready to leave Albany. Divisional flagships cleared the harbor first, so as to assume their rightful places of command. By 1700 hours, the people of Albany had jammed the water's edge for their last glimpse of the American battleships. They counted fourteen, as *Missouri* and *Connecticut* were still coaling. The former was delayed for three hours, while the latter was unable to depart until after midnight. The flagship caught up to the fleet later that same day.

Sperry's task force rounded the southern tip of Western Australia and pushed north through the Indian Ocean. The flagship set the pace at eleven knots. And this pace is what concerned Admiral Sperry. The fleet was on a time-table much like a train schedule. Arrival and departure times from scheduled ports-of-call were based on such factors as speed and distance to each destination, time allotted for each visit, and refueling requirements. In all this Admiral Sperry had to be mindful of the endurance of Admiral Schroeder's Fourth Division. This division contained the ships with the least bunker capacity. These included Schroeder's flagship *Wisconsin,* with *Illinois, Kearsarge,* and *Kentucky.* Ships running short of fuel in mid ocean were the greatest threat to the timetable. So Sperry ordered Schroeder to reduce speed to nine knots so as to conserve fuel. This caused Fourth Division to lag behind and eventually lose sight of the main body.

On September 26, the fleet was off Java. A halt was called before the Lombok Strait. The narrow fissure of water was socked in by fog. When it cleared, the advance continued past Bali and into the Java Sea.

A combination of calm seas and adroit cruise control enabled Fourth Division to gain ground on the main body. By the time Schroeder's column had sliced through the Lombok Strait it was only thirty miles astern Sperry's force. The two columns cut north across the Java Sea for the Makassar Strait, swept through the passage that separates Borneo from Celebes, and pushed into the Celebes Sea.

Fourth Division linked up with the main body on September 30 off the Philippines. *Connecticut* led the single column up the Basilan Strait to Zamboanga. As the battleships sailed by the largest city on Mindanao, they loosed a thunderous salute with their twelve-inch guns.

The battlewagons continued north through the Sulu Sea. They surged past Palawan and broke into the South China Sea, then round Mindoro for Luzon. On October 2, lookouts spotted Corregidor. The Great White Fleet had reached Manila Bay.

The importance of the Philippines to American strategy in the Pacific can readily be seen on a map. The Philippines lie south of Formosa (Taiwan) and north of the Dutch East Indies (Indonesia). To the west is the South China Sea and to the east is the Philippine Sea. From Luzon, the United States could cut off any Japanese thrust into the South Pacific. This made the Great White Fleet's visit to the Philippines one of the most crucial during the entire cruise.

But Manila's importance to America's Pacific strategy meant little to the Filipinos. Their interest was in preparing for the more than fourteen thousand visitors who were going to spend a lot of money in their city. Indeed the whole town was fit to bust out. Preparations were extensive and buckets of money had been spent, over $120,000. But it was all for naught. For Manila was caught in the grips of a cholera epidemic. Six years before, the disease had ravaged the islands, killing more than sixty thousand people. And now it was back to wreak more terrible havoc. Orders came down from the commander-in-chief: Crews would be restricted to their ships during the fleet's entire stay in port.

With the prospect of liberty denied, it was important that the crews were kept busy. Officers assigned duties to ready the ships for the next port-of-call. As usual, the most important of these tasks was that of refueling. For the next eight days, ships took turns taking on coal. The next stop was Yokohama, and no provisions had been made to refuel in Japan, so more coal than usual was taken on. Bunkers were filled to capacity. Eight hundred-pound bags of coal were piled high on the decks. Each ship, it was thought, had enough coal to make it back to Manila. For it was decided that the fleet would make its official visit to the Philippine capital after the stopover in Japan;

provided, of course, that the epidemic had run its course. So the Philippine Government began an energetic campaign to eradicate the disease so as to ensure the return of the fleet.

On October 4, southern Luzon was attacked by a typhoon. The hundred mile-per-hour winds put a stop to the coaling operations, but only briefly, as refueling was quickly resumed. Word that another typhoon was in the offing caused a day's delay in sailing. However, with a schedule to keep, the fleet would sail regardless on October 10.

At 0600 hours, the fleet steamed out of Manila. The ships skirted the west coast of Luzon, heading north through the South China Sea. The sun was warm and reassuring. The sea was mild as milk. Men sunbathed on the decks. Others read, while some just gazed out to sea.

Suddenly, barometers plunged. Skies became black. Seas rose, then became turbulent. By the morning of October 12, the second typhoon had struck with all its fury. Ships became scattered, tossed about the angry seas like flotsam. Some cut their engines and rode the peaks and troughs of mountainous waves. Water, tons of it, crashed over bridges and superstructures. Lifeboats in their davits were smashed to matchwood. Bags of coal were tossed into the sea. Those on watch hung on for dear life. Atop *Kearsarge,* angry seas ripped out the antenna and foretopmast and flung them over the side. Three men from *Rhode Island* were washed overboard. Two were plucked from the maelstrom. But gunner's mate William Fuller could not be saved. His would-be rescuers watched helplessly as their comrade was tossed about like a cork, then swallowed up by the hungry seas.

On the 13th, the seas relented. Skies cleared. Scattered units were recalled. Damage was assessed and repairs were made. Sperry shuffled the pack and dealt again, until something resembling a task force plied across the placid seas. The storm had forced a twenty-four-hour delay in the fleet's arrival at Yokohama. Wireless transmissions notified the Japanese of the change in schedule. It made little difference in Tokyo. On time or late, the Japanese were ready and eager to welcome Teddy Roosevelt's Great White Fleet.

The Japanese had planned many months for the Americans' visit, and anticipation in the Land of the Rising Sun was at fever pitch. In spite of the ill-will that existed between the burgeoning Pacific powers, the Japanese were going full tilt to make the Americans' visit a memorable one. Besides, there was the all important issue of saving face: Tokyo and Yokohama were not going to be outdone by Melbourne and Sydney.

On October 18, the Great White Fleet was off Yokohama. It did not take long for the Americans to see that the welcome mat was out. *Connecticut's* wireless operator became inundated with a blizzard of welcome signals. Cruisers *Mogami, Tatsuta, Soya,* and six merchant-men sidled up as escorts. Standing out boldly on the black hulls of the Japanese steamers were large white letters that spelled *Welcome.* The decks were crammed with soldiers and civilians, among them women and children, waving Japanese and American flags and singing American patriotic songs.

Tokyo Bay was blanketed in a heavy mist. The sun

burned away the veil of moisture to reveal the Japanese escorts entering the bay. Close astern were the American battleships. The visitors were ushered to an anchorage specially prepared for them. Sperry's task force shared Tokyo Bay with many of the heavy units of the Imperial Navy. In keeping with the spirit of the occasion, American and Japanese battleships traded thunderous volleys of salute.

Of all the nations on the globetrotters' schedule, Japan presented the greatest challenge with regards to the observance of the social graces. So concerned was the White House with potential indiscretions that President Roosevelt favored restricting American enlisted personnel to their ships for the entire time the fleet was in port. Admiral Sperry cautioned that such action was premature and that bluejackets and marines should be allowed to go ashore to see the sights and enjoy any entertainment that had been planned for them. And besides, the host might just take offense. The Japanese were well aware of the lengths to which the Australians and New Zealanders went to make the Americans feel at home. Tokyo would never forgive Washington if it was not afforded the opportunity to do the same.

This prompted Admiral Sperry to write Henry Denison. Sperry had met Denison while at The Hague, when the latter was acting as a representative for the Japanese Government at the International Court of Arbitration. This unusual American was from Guildhall, Vermont. After receiving his degree in law at George Washington University, Denison was assigned as a vice consul at the American Consulate in Yokohama. The young American diplomat so impressed the Japanese that they asked him to be their legal advisor in the Ministry of Foreign Affairs.

Denison held this position for thirty-three years and was instrumental in such important diplomatic initiatives as the treaty concluding the Chinese-Japanese War of 1894–95, the Treaty of Friendship with Great Britain, and a treaty ending the Russo-Japanese War of 1904–05. In fact, Denison accompanied Ambassador Baron Komura to Portsmouth, New Hampshire, in 1905 to meet with President Theodore Roosevelt and the Russian dignitaries for the signing of the treaty. Because of his invaluable services, the Japanese Government later awarded Denison the Grand Cordon of the Rising Sun. This was a particularly singular honor since Denison was the first foreigner to earn the decoration.

Sperry outlined in detail the needs of the fleet for the visit. Denison forwarded Sperry's letter to those Japanese naval officers responsible for arranging the American visit. Denison's legwork proved instrumental in assuring that the fleet's visit to Japan was one of the most successful of the entire cruise.

Yet the navy was not going to take any chances. Drunkenness would not be tolerated. Officers incurring indiscretions were liable for court martial. On the Japanese side, everything that could be done by the Foreign Office and Law Enforcement was done to handle any situation that might arise due to American ignorance of Japanese customs.

At 1400 hours, on the day of the fleet's arrival, Admiral Sperry went ashore. He attended a garden party given in his honor by the city officials of Yokohama. Officers and ratings who had been allowed ashore were paraded through the streets of Tokyo. Many of those lining the parade route cheered and waved Japanese and American flags. Many of the Americans ended up at Uraga, where more than fifty years before Commodore Perry made his historic landing.

The next day, Monday, October 19, was proclaimed American Day in Tokyo. Over one thousand school children welcomed Admiral Sperry and his entourage. Sperry and his officers were then made the official guests of the emperor. Sperry, his flag officers, and their aides were accommodated at the Shiba Detached Palace. All battleship skippers were quartered at the Imperial Hotel.

On the 20th, Sperry and his command attended a luncheon as the honored guests of the emperor himself. The following day, the Americans attended a garden party hosted by none other than Admiral Heihachiro Togo, hero of the historic Japanese victory at Tsushima Strait. The reception was held in the Shinjuki Imperial Gardens. This was no small honor, for these were the private gardens of the empress. The reception held for the Americans was just the second time that the gardens had been made available for public use. The first was following Togo's victory over the Russian Navy.

Like a bad penny, the coal situation again reared its ugly head. Because of the typhoon, the fleet had burned more fuel than was planned; plus, many of the bags of extra coal that had been piled on the decks of the battleships were now lying at the bottom of the Pacific. Fortunately, the U.S. Navy had a small coal depot in Yokohama. With assistance from the Japanese, 3,500 tons of coal was made available to the American ships and parceled out where needed.

On the 23rd, their last day as the official guests of the emperor, the Americans attended a luncheon at the Shiba

Detached Palace. That evening, American flag officers and battleship skippers were honored with a lavish dinner aboard the battleship *Fuji*. This was immediately followed up by a reception aboard the battleship *Mikasa*, Togo's flagship at Tsushima Strait. Wine and champagne flowed like water. In short order, both hosts and guests were pretty well inebriated. Many of the latter were actually hoisted on the shoulders of the former and carried round the decks of the historic *Mikasa*. Fortunately, no brawls broke out and no one was lost over the side.

The next day, the Americans decided to return the favor. A lavish dinner and reception was planned for that evening aboard *Connecticut*. And it was here that the only faux pas during the entire visit occurred. The event was planned for 3,500 guests. Trouble ensued when many more showed up, and a good number of these arrived early. This caused a shortage of food. Blame was placed squarely on the caterers, though the fact that less than $1,500 had been earmarked for the affair just might have had something to do with it as well. One can imagine how this lack of preparation was received by the customs-conscious Japanese.

The American fleet was due to depart on October 25. Thousands of curious Japanese lined the water's edge to see the visitors off. A party of Japanese dignitaries, led by the Minister of Foreign Affaires, was piped aboard *Connecticut*. Full honors were accorded the visitors. The departure ceremony of speeches and salutes was brief. After the Japanese officials had taken their leave, the fleet prepared to sail. On signal from the flagship, all battleships got up steam and weighed anchor. *Connecticut* assumed her rightful place at the head of First Squadron. The Japanese cruisers *Katori, Ikoma, Kashima,* and *Tsukuba* joined up as escort.

The American ships entered the inner harbor. The crews of the Japanese warships passed along the way cheered mightily for the departing occidental visitors. Aboard the Yankee battleships, bands replied with Japan's National Anthem. At a pre-arranged point in the inner harbor, each battlewagon came about smartly and headed for the open sea. As the last American ship exited the inner harbor, the escorting Japanese cruisers loosed a volley in salute. This signaled the end of the historic visit of the Great White Fleet to the Land of the Rising Sun.

Politically, Japan was the most sensitive port-of-call during the entire cruise. This fact was clearly understood on both sides of the Pacific when Japan presented its invitation. In the five years leading up to the visit, such issues as emigration, the growing naval competition, and the imperialist ambitions of Tokyo and Washington all manifested themselves in an air of suspicion and distrust.

Admiral Sperry sent a wireless to President Roosevelt, telling him that the visit was a resounding success. He added that the Japanese had treated himself and his men with extraordinary courtesy. Roosevelt was extremely pleased. He interpreted the success to a combination of fellowship and the demonstration of American power as exemplified by his Great White Fleet.

The visit did much to dispel the tension that existed between Washington and Tokyo. The day after the fleet's departure, Japan's ambassador in Washington, Takahira Kagoro, communicated Tokyo's desire to iron out differences with the United States. At the end of November, the Japanese ambassador and Elihu Root, the American

Secretary of State, signed the Root-Takahira Agreement. Now each nation would respect the other's position in the Pacific. China's independence and territorial integrity would be assured and the Open Door Policy would be allowed to continue. Both nations agreed to consultations to smooth out any future crises in the Pacific.

The Root-Takahira Agreement succeeded in muting much of the harsh rhetoric that was often swapped like broadsides back and forth across the Pacific. A new reality seemed to take shape, one in which the United States recognized Japan's aggrandizement of Korea and Tokyo's growing influence in Manchuria. In Japanese eyes, this made up—at least in part—for the American failure to broker reparations for the Japanese following Japan's defeat of czarist forces in the Russo-Japanese War of 1904–05. By 1908, it was plain to see that Japan was pursuing her version of the Monroe Doctrine in the Far East. Tokyo, though, was much more proactive in its attempt at economic dominance in the Far East than was the United States in South America. Indeed it was to prove the forerunner of the later Japanese militarists' doctrine known as the Greater East Asia Co-Prosperity Sphere.

Yet in the end, the Root-Takahira Agreement or something of a comparable nature would have been consummated regardless, for Japan's economy was under pressure. Increased military budgets were the major culprit. Such was the high cost of imperialism by attempting to keep up with the Joneses. In fact, by 1908, Japan's budget deficit was nearly 5 million yen.

But help was on the way and from an unexpected quarter: The American Congress. The legislative body saw fit to cut in half the battleship construction targets that had been put forth by the White House. Japan saw this as an opportunity to work out its economic problems with Washington. After all, Japan's strained economy was the major cause of Japanese emigration to the United States. During the growing rapprochement that followed, Japanese emigration was cut back.

Yet there was an underlying current of distrust that proved resistant to cordial relations. When Japanese and American naval planners prepared war games, it was with each other's fleets in mind. Both realized that Russian naval power in the Pacific was broken; that the major units of the German Navy lacked the range to be effective; that the Royal Navy had pulled back to oppose the growing German threat in the North Sea. This left Japan and the United States, both relative newcomers to the imperialist ranks, as the preeminent naval powers in the world's largest ocean. Japan recognized that the Great White Fleet was an orchestrated demonstration of America's ability to transfer naval power from the Atlantic to the Pacific. The Japanese clearly saw, too, that the United States was beginning to fortify Corregidor in the Philippines; that it would do likewise on Guam; that the United States Navy was developing Hawaii as a major base; that the United States, Australia, and New Zealand were forming a coalition of white, Anglo- Saxon powers in the Pacific. The last named proved a major issue in the platform of the Fascist ideology espoused by the militarists in their rise to power during the 1920s and 30s.

However, for the time being, Japan and the United States seemed to have ameliorated the discord that threatened to bring them to blows. Yet in the wake of improving relations, rumors continued to circulate of a German-American-Chinese Alliance.

The Japanese knew full well that the American fleet was going to call on China after leaving the Home Islands. They were cognizant, too, of German machinations to spoil the budding Japanese-American relationship. This included the dissemination of such fictions as Japanese sabotage of the American battleships while on the world cruise; or that Japan was going to land troops in Mexico or Latin America. Kaiser Wilhelm had wanted, in 1907, an alliance with the United States and China, with the aim of keeping alive the Open Door Policy. However, the reality was quite different. Germany was looking to improve its position in China, while at the same time undermine Britain's strategic position in the Atlantic by subverting a possible alliance with the United States.

However, Teddy Roosevelt was smarter than the average bear. He understood the German position very well. And the kaiser did little to dispel that understanding. In June 1908, the kaiser granted an interview with William B. Hale of the *New York Times*. In the course of the interview, the kaiser issued several notable prognostications. He predicted that India would revolt against British rule that winter; that Germany and Britain would go to war in the not-to-distant future; that Japan and the United States would also come to blows; and he assured Hale that the United States would have the full support of the German Empire in such a conflict and that China's territorial integrity would be assured against encroachments by Japan.

Hale understood the gravity of the emperor's remarks. He took his notes to the American ambassador in Berlin.

The diplomat urged the suppression of the notes, though he did show them to the German foreign minister. The German minister, too, understood the gravity of his monarch's remarks. The notes found their way to President Roosevelt, who concurred with his ambassador that they were not publication. Roosevelt eventually forwarded the notes to Lord Balfour.

Such prognostications from Berlin served to reinforce Roosevelt's belief as to why the Germans were the greater threat. The president was going to make sure that the United States was not going to be drawn into an Anglo-American showdown. He also was going to make sure that the United States was not going to be sucked into fighting the Japanese in China at the behest of Germany. Such a development, he knew, would give rise to a British-French-Japanese-Russian alliance, an association Germany, America, and China could not hope to defeat.

Such was the gravity of the Hale interview that it wound up being shelved until the early 1930s. Yet the kaiser failed to grasp the obvious signs of the American-Japanese rapprochement: The success of the Great White Fleet's visit to Tokyo and Yokohama, and the Root-Takahira Agreement and the decline of Japanese emigration. Following the Great White Fleet's return to Hampton Roads in February 1909, Washington was under no illusions as to where the major strategic threat lay. From 1909 to the outbreak of war in 1914, the bulk of the American battleship force was concentrated in the Atlantic.

For the short term at least, President Roosevelt and his Great White Fleet were able to relieve tensions in the Far East; put a stopper in the bottle of German attempts to manipulate American foreign policy; and forge an Anglo-American association that has endured to the present day.

THERE'S NO PLACE LIKE HOME

Early in the morning of October 27, the fleet split into two groups. First Battleship Squadron, under Rear Admiral Sperry, sailed on for the Philippines. Second Battleship Squadron, under Rear Admiral Emory, steamed for China.

If the visit to Japan caused the most anxiety, then the visit to China proved the most fruitless. The importance attached to the stopovers in New Zealand, Australia, and Japan reflected Washington's agenda for America as a major power on the Pacific Rim. In consequence, the China visit was downplayed. Japan was the most important stop on the Pacific itinerary for the political and military reasons previously discussed. And these concerns carried over in the visit to China. To alleviate Japanese suspicions, Washington decided that only half the Great White Fleet would call on China. To further placate Tokyo, the ships would put into the backwater port of Amoy. This caused Chinese enthusiasm for the visit to wane. The Realpolitik of the imperialists' agenda dashed the cup of hope from expectant lips: There would be no German-American-Chinese alliance to oppose Japan. So Peking accepted the inevitable and made preparations for the incoming eight American battleships.

To accommodate the visitors, an entertainment compound had to be built from scratch. An army of coolies was organized for the task. They worked round the clock until everything was in readiness for when the Americans came to call. But then there ensued a string of events that served to add to the pessimism and despair that were already clouding the Americans' visit. It started with the Chinese, who suddenly began leaving Amoy in droves. Rumors had begun to circulate that Amoy was to be an American base of operations for actions against the Japanese in China. A government proclamation was issued to counter the stories, but the exodus continued. In the end, authorities had to resort to draconian methods to keep the Chinese from deserting. Then a typhoon slammed into Amoy, the same storm that had lashed the American fleet on its way to Japan. The blow killed three thousand people and laid waste to the newly erected entertainment compound. Work began at once and the facilities were repaired in time for the fleet's visit. Next came a threat from a group of Chinese revolutionaries, an alleged plot that involved the assassination of Chinese officials. Chinese soldiers and security personnel swept down on Amoy, closing off the town and isolating the compound.

American Minister to China William M. Rockhill added to the pervading gloom that was enveloping Amoy. In an effort to further diminish the political importance of the fleet's visit, Rockhill decided not to be on hand as a representative of the American legation. He would send his military attaché in his place.

Before the American ships arrived, the gunboat, *Niobe,* put into Amoy. This allegedly was a coal stop for the German ship. But when the American battleships arrived two weeks later, on October 30, *Niobe* was still in port. For the Americans, the German presence only added to the air of gloom and suspicion that already smothered the compound. While there as enough food, drink, and entertainment to go round, there was something conspicuously absent: The great crush of people. The wildly delirious throngs that greeted the Americans at nearly every port-of-call was missing in Amoy. With all the soldiers and security personnel on hand, the visitors' entertainment compound seemed more like a prison camp.

While in port, the American fleet paid homage to the dowager empress on her birthday. Every ship was fully dressed and flew Chinese ensigns. Twenty-one-gun salutes set fire to the night and the ensigns were bathed in searchlights. This was one of the last celebrations enjoyed by the dowager empress. She died shortly afterwards.

The American ships left Amoy on November 5. As the task force steamed out of the Formosa Strait, *Louisiana* detached and sped for Hong Kong. The rest of Second Battleship Squadron continued on for the Philippines. *Louisiana* lifted Rear Admiral Emory to the British colony so he could begin his journey home and retirement. Rear Admiral Schroeder, commander of Fourth Battleship Division, was promoted to command Second Battleship Squadron. This made him subordinate commander of the Great White Fleet. Captain William P. Potter of *Vermont* was promoted to flag rank. He assumed command of Fourth Battleship Division. In Potter's place, Captain Frank F. Fletcher became the new skipper of the Green Mountain State battleship.

When the Great White Fleet split up after leaving Japan, First Battleship Squadron went directly to the Philippines. It arrived at Subic Bay on October 31. Second Battleship

Squadron arrived from China on November 7. The scheduled stay of the fleet was three weeks. During that time, Admiral Sperry put his crews through their paces with range calibration exercises and battle practice drills. The ships were also fueled and provisioned for the next leg of the cruise. In between, the crews took turns going ashore. Liberty is a great release for a sailor. It can provide plenty of diversions from the drudgery of duty or from long periods at sea. But in the Philippines, the sailors and marines of the Great White Fleet very nearly missed getting liberty.

Admiral Sperry was against his men going ashore. This was not to say that he was opposed to the idea of liberty. As a career navy man, nobody understood what the occasional release from duty did for a sailor like Admiral Sperry. But Manila recently had been in the throes of a cholera epidemic, and he had no desire to have his crews infected. The American governor-general of the islands disagreed and contacted Secretary of War William Taft. Taft, in turn, contacted Secretary of the Navy Newberry. Newberry cabled Sperry, urging him to reconsider. He added that President Roosevelt ordered him to discuss the subject of liberty with the governor-general. In the end, Sperry acquiesced. But he laid out strict rules for cleanliness to limit the potential for another outbreak.

Before the Great White Fleet departed the Philippines, it swapped a number of sailors and marines with the Asiatic Squadron. Nearly 150 officers and non-commissioned officers and more than a thousand ratings were exchanged. Then, on December 1, 1908, *Connecticut* led the fleet out of Manila Bay.

The American ships cut south through the South China

Sea, past the Spratly Islands, toward the tip of Malaysia. By December 6, the fleet was off Singapore. Lying in wait was an armada of small craft. The American battleships steamed by in review. *Connecticut* fired a twenty-one-gun salute to the British ensign.

Sperry's task force rounded the Malay Peninsula and pushed north, up into the Malacca Strait. On the second night in the sliver of water that separates Sumatra and Malaysia, *New Jersey* signaled men overboard. All ships stopped. Boats were launched and searchlights probed the darkness. One man was plucked from the black waters, but the fleet could not wait. It moved on, leaving *New Jersey* to continue the search. Three hours later, the battle-wagon recovered all boats and left the scene without having located its missing crewman.

On December 9, the fleet broke into the Andaman Sea. That evening, a seaman aboard *Georgia* was diagnosed with smallpox. The battleship broke formation and proceeded with all possible dispatch to Ceylon (Sri Lanka). The rest of the ship's crew who had gone ashore in Manila was inoculated.

Meanwhile, the main body of the fleet continued to slice across the Bay of Bengal. The weather was fair. The sea was like a mill pond. The fleet arrived off Ceylon at 2300 hours on December 12. It rounded Pointe de Galle and there dropped anchor. In the morning, harbor pilots assisted with the fleet's entrance into Colombo. *Georgia* was reunited with the fleet.

The fleet was due to stay in Colombo for a week. Very little in the way of entertainment had been planned. Nevertheless, some bluejackets and marines managed to get ashore. Liberty was restricted to between the hours of 1300 to 1800—enough time to take in the shops and beaches, get a tattoo, or scout up feminine companionship. Officers attended a number of dinners, banquets, and receptions. The highlight affair was a reception given by the colonial-governor, Sir Henry E. McCallum, for Admiral Sperry and all flag and commanding officers. Sperry had been McCallum's house guest for several days and the duo presided over several such social functions.

The main reason for the layover in Colombo was to coal and provision. The distance from Manila to the Suez Canal was beyond the range of the American ships. So a pit stop was necessary. Thankfully, this time there was no disruption in fuel supplies. The trio of colliers that had been contracted was actually waiting in the harbor when the American fleet arrived in Colombo.

The fleet departed Colombo on December 20. The weather was balmy. The Arabian Sea was smooth as glass. Just the conditions for drills. The daily regimen consisted of battle drills, signal drills, range-finding drills, searchlight drills, and maneuvers. To break the tension of the constant exercises, the crews of each ship came up with a number of diversions. For instance, aboard *Connecticut*, the ship's orchestra assembled each evening on the quarter deck for sixty-minute concerts.

The island of Socotra was sighted the day after Christmas. The fleet filtered into the Gulf of Aden, skirted the tip of Yemen, and pushed into the Red Sea. The American fleet passed heavy traffic moving south. Among the traffic was a British troopship bound for India. Many of the Tommies had gathered on deck to catch a glimpse of the American battleships plodding northwards. Many of the king's own traded hails of encouragement with the passing Yanks. As the last ship in line passed by, the British soldiers all gave the fleet three rousing cheers.

On January 3, 1909, the American ships had reached the northern rim of the Red Sea. Sperry called a halt and there the fleet dropped anchor. The Great White Fleet had reached the Suez Canal. It was two days ahead of schedule.

The Great White Fleet was the largest group of ships to ever transit the Suez Canal up to that time. This forced a closing of the Canal to all other traffic to accommodate Sperry's task force. The American battleships were split into three groups. Each group was allotted a day to transit the Canal. *Connecticut* led the first group through. Five ships made the passage on the second day. *Georgia* spearheaded the last group. However, *Georgia* ran aground near Bitter Lakes. It took two hours to free the Peach Tree State Battleship, but she resumed her place at the head of her group and led them to Port Said.

Port Said was a coaling stop. The Egyptian port was not large enough to handle all of Sperry's battleships at the same time, so plans called for the refueling of each group as it arrived. It was expected that each group would be refueled and out of the harbor in time for the arrival of the next group. However, like the best-laid plans of mice and men, the tight coaling schedule quickly fell apart.

The company supplying the coal brought their colliers into the harbor one at a time. This slowed refueling operations. Then the Americans accused the supplier of trying to shortchange them on the agreed amount. The company denied the accusation. The resulting dispute nearly brought refueling operations to a halt. However, cooler heads prevailed and coaling operations were allowed to proceed. But because it had taken so long to coal, Admiral Sperry had to revise his Mediterranean timetable.

It was now impossible for the Great White Fleet to call on each and every port slated for a visit as it was originally planned. At the same time, the State and Navy Departments had no wish to insult the governments involved by ringing up cancellations. So an alternative plan was drawn up. Instead of the fleet halving itself into squadrons, it would subdivide into divisions. First Division was to proceed to Italy, then on to Villefranche and the French Riviera. Second Division was to make for Marseilles. Third Division was to scatter and call on Greek and Turkish ports, while Fourth Division was to hop, skip, and jump to Malta, Tripoli, and Algiers.

Before it left Egypt, First Division had its itinerary amended. This was called for because Sicily and southern Italy had been wracked by an earthquake and tidal wave. Initial estimates put the death toll at a whopping 200,000. Admiral Sperry ordered the auxiliary *Culgoa* there to render assistance. Then he ordered that any medical supplies that could be spared were to be loaded aboard the *Yankton*. A half a dozen surgeons were sent packing as well, and the auxiliary made for the scene of disaster at flank speed.

On January 5, Admiral Sperry in the battleship *Connecticut* left Port Said for Messina. The rest of First Division—*Vermont, Kansas,* and *Minnesota*—steamed for Villefranche. *Connecticut* arrived at the disaster area on January 9. Bluejackets from the flagship went ashore to help clear debris, dig out survivors, and unload supplies from the *Culgoa*. A detachment of *Connecticut* petty officers formed a guard of honor at the funeral services of the wife of the British consul. The next day *Connecticut* departed, lifting the American Ambassador to Italy Lloyd C. Griscom to Naples. The flagship remained in the Italian port for the next ten days, directing the American relief efforts. Sperry ordered *Illinois,* en route to Malta with *Kearsarge* and *Wisconsin,* to break off and make all possible speed to Messina to render assistance. The battleship arrived on January 14. For the next two days, seamen from the ship joined those from *Yankton* and *Scorpion* to uncover the bodies of the American consul and his wife from the rubble of the American consulate. When this grim task was completed, *Illinois* sailed for Malta to rejoin *Kearsarge* and *Wisconsin.*

Before *Connecticut* left Italy, Admiral Sperry was granted an audience with King Victor Emmanuel in Rome. The monarch extended his personal gratitude for American assistance during the crisis. Meanwhile, the rest of the fleet conducted its whirlwind tour of the Mediterranean.

On January 6, Rear Admiral Schroeder with *Louisiana* and *Virginia* departed Port Said for Beirut and then Smyrna, arriving at the latter on January 11. The other two ships of Third Division, *Ohio* and *Missouri,* left Port Said two days later, arriving at Athens on January 11. King George of Greece hosted a dinner party for the officers on January 17. The next day, the warships steamed for Salonica, arriving January 19. Following a two-day stay, *Ohio* and *Missouri* sailed for Smyrna, arriving the next day. Third Division remained until January 25, when it made for Gibraltar, arriving at The Rock on February 1.

On January 7, Rear Admiral Potter of Fourth Division

attended a dinner given for him and his officers by the khedive of Egypt and Sir Eldon Gorst of the British Foreign Office at the khedive's palace. The following day, *Kentucky* sailed for Tripoli, while on the 10th, *Illinois, Kearsarge,* and *Wisconsin* headed for Malta. The former made her detour to Messina on the 11th, but rejoined her sisters at Malta six days later. On the 19th, the trio left for Algiers, arriving on the 21st. They were reunited with *Kentucky,* which had arrived from Tripoli three days later. Fourth Division then left Algiers on the thirtieth, arriving at Gibraltar on February 1.

Of Admiral Wainwright's Second Division, *Georgia* and *Nebraska* left Port Said for Marseilles on January 8. *New Jersey* and *Rhode Island* followed suit the next day. *Georgia* and *Nebraska* arrived at Marseilles on the 14th. *New Jersey* and *Rhode Island* pulled in two days later. *Georgia* and *Nebraska* left the French port on the 27th and stopped at Tangiers on the 30th. They left the next day for the short steam to Gibraltar. *New Jersey* and *Rhode Island,* having departed Marseilles on the 28th, joined their sisters at The Rock on February 1.

First Battleship Division arrived at Gibraltar on January 31, 1909. Crowds had gathered at numerous vantage points on The Rock to view the spectacle. In the harbor awaiting the American warships were the British battleships *Albemarle* and *Albion* and the Second Cruiser Squadron. Representing the Russian Navy were the battleships *Tsarevitch* and *Slava* and the cruisers *Oleg* and *Bogatyr.* There were gunboats from France and Holland. Each ship greeted the travelers with decks manned and bands playing. *Connecticut* loosed a volley while she passed in review. It was answered by *Albemarle* and batteries ashore. Vice Admiral Goodrich, RN, graciously called on Admiral Sperry first. It was a classy gesture for the Great White Fleet's final port-of-call.

The five-day visit was a coaling stop, some 1,500 tons per vessel. But time was allotted, too, for rest and relaxation. Unlike at Port-of-Spain, here the British proved to be excellent hosts. American sailors and marines fraternized with their British counterparts in a plethora of games and festivities. Especially popular and competitive were the rowing events and boxing matches. However, for one man, Gibraltar would not be a place of fond memories.

Edward Francis Qualtrough was a career naval officer. He graduated from the Naval Academy at Annapolis in 1871. He became an ardent champion among the growing movement of naval officers pressing their case for a strong navy. In 1889, he went public with his ideas in the magazine *Overland Monthly*. There he elaborated on the weakness of America's coastal defenses and the need for Congress to allocate the appropriate funds to build a navy powerful enough to deter the growing number of imperialist powers. This, and other expressions of such policy, propelled Qualtrough through the ranks and put him in good stead in certain areas of Capitol Hill.

Qualtrough was assigned to the round-the-world cruise when the Great White Fleet put into San Francisco. He assumed command of the battleship *Georgia*. *Georgia* was the flagship of Rear Admiral Wainwright of the Second Battleship Division. This was indeed an opportunity for eventual advancement to flag rank. However, by the time the Great White Fleet reached the Mediterranean, Captain Qualtrough was slated for court-martial.

The incident leading to the court-martial occurred in Tangier. The United States Minister to Morocco, Samuel N. Grummere, had hosted a ball. Earlier in the day, Captain Qualtrough had attended a tea. He is alleged to have returned to his ship somewhat inebriated. Later at the ball, he appeared to be, according to those in attendance, quite unsteady of gait. Admiral Wainwright relieved the skipper of his command. At the hearing, Qualtrough claimed that long hours on the bridge of his command combined with little food or rest had taken its toll. The ship's surgeon testified that Captain Qualtrough was in ill health and that he had treated the commander for gastric catarrh. Qualtrough did admit to having one drink, but added that it was the cigar he had smoked that had induced his seemingly drunken condition. However, Admiral Wainwright and five other officers saw things differently and testified to their brother officer's intoxicated condition. The court-martial board did not see it that way and ruled in Captain Qualtrough's favor. Admiral Sperry, though, did not. Qualtrough was relieved of his command and restricted to his ship for the rest of the voyage. His place was taken by Lieutenant-Commander George F. Kline. Qualtrough left the Navy on June 30, 1909.

February 6, 1909, was the day of departure. The sky was clear and the sea was like glass. The American battleships got up steam and by 0900 began to edge out of the harbor. Wainwright's Second Division led the exodus. *Georgia* was out in front, with *Nebraska, New Jersey,* and *Rhode Island* astern. As the visitors slowly made their way out of the harbor, bands aboard the Royal Navy ships played songs like, "For He's a Jolly Good Fellow" and "Auld Lang Syne."

By 1030 hours, fifteen battlewagons—their props slowly churning the waters of Gibraltar and their stacks spewing thick funnels of black smoke—waited in a single-line formation for the flagship. Vice Admiral Goodrich, flying his flag aboard HMS *Devonshire*, ordered a twenty-one gun salute to the departing *Connecticut*. The *Devonshire's* band struck up the "Star-Spangled Banner." *Connecticut* returned the gesture with her own thunderous salute to the British ensign. Then the flagship's band took up "God Save the King."

Connecticut passed along the stone white hulls to take her place at the head of the line. The sixteen American battleships slowly made their way out into the Atlantic. In the background, echoing from the British bastion, were the familiar strains of "Home Sweet Home." The Great White Fleet had made its final port-of-call. It was going home.

The homestretch drive across the Atlantic was not going to be a milk run. Admiral Sperry had intended to keep his crews on their toes with exercises and drills. He also planned to board each battleship for the annual admiral's inspection. But the Atlantic refused to cooperate. High winds and heavy seas made drills and inspections all but impossible. For three days, Sperry's task force rode the washboard that was the Atlantic Ocean.

The weather relented on February 10. The fleet got in a full day's drills before the weather again soured. So the drills were curtailed. Meanwhile, back in the States, a squadron was put together to meet the globetrotters. The new battleships *New Hampshire*, *Mississippi*, and *Idaho*, Atlantic Fleet Flagship *Maine*, with two armored and three scout cruisers, left Hampton Roads on February 14.

In command was Rear Admiral Conway H. Arnold. The two forces made the link up in the Atlantic three days later on the 17th. The way was now clear for the fleet's triumphal return.

Swarming like moths around a searchlight on a summer night, people flocked to Hampton Roads in their tens of thousands. "No Vacancy" signs were everywhere, as hotels, inns, and rooming houses became jammed. Bunting and streamers grew like jungle vegetation overnight. Chesapeake Bay became a parking lot of yachts and steamers. On hand was the navy yacht *Dolphin*, with House and Senate Naval Affairs Committee members aboard. The presidential yacht *Mayflower* hovered nearby, with President Roosevelt and Secretary of the Navy Newberry. In cities like Norfolk, Richmond, and Baltimore, entertainment of every variety and stripe awaited the sailors and marines of the Great White Fleet.

On February 21, the fleet was off Cape May, New Jersey. Here it would anchor for the night. Following Secretary Newberry's orders, Sperry's task force would not make its triumphal entry until the next day. And it was fitting that it should be so, for the next day was George Washington's birthday.

February 22, 1909, dawned cloudy with intermittent rainsqualls. A fleet of small craft awaited the battleships off Tail-of-the-Horseshoe-Lightship. About 1100 hours, masts and superstructures appeared through the curtain of mist. Twenty-six men-of-war, all led by *Connecticut*, steamed in a seven-mile-long column. On signal, the task force loosed a thunderous twenty-one-gun barrage.

The column bore down on the presidential yacht. As each ship passed in review, it rendered a twenty-one-gun salute to the flag of the commander-in-chief. With each volley, an eruption of bells and whistles sounded from the armada of small craft. As the last ship in the column passed, *Mayflower* fell astern and trailed the fleet into Hampton Roads.

Battleship *Connecticut* steamed past Fort Monroe off Old Point Comfort. Thousands of well-wishers braved the rain, waving and cheering as they welcomed the crews home. In the distance, a band played "There's No Place Like Home."

When the fleet was finally at anchor, a reception was held aboard the *Mayflower* for the flag officers and battleship skippers. This was followed up by the president visiting the flagship of each division. On board *Connecticut,* he addressed the crew, praising them for their accomplishment. To those assembled on the flagship's afterdeck, he said, "Others may do as you have done, but they'll have to follow you."[1]

With those words, the round-the-world cruise was officially over. The greatest circumnavigation of the globe in modern maritime history now belonged to the ages. In one of its finest hours, the United States Navy changed the course of history and did so without firing a single shot in anger. And because of the triumph of the Great White Fleet, the United States, for better or worse, truly became a global power.

POSTSCRIPT

The Pribilof Islands lie in the Bering Sea, just north of the Aleutian Chain. For years, the islands were a Mecca for poachers who took a heavy toll of the seal population there. On July 16–17, 1906, Japanese poachers landed for another harvest of skins. This time they were surprised by an American patrol, and in the ensuing skirmish five of the intruders were killed. This incident, little remembered now, was one of many at the time that ratcheted up the tensions between Japan and the United States.

Japan was a rising star in the fraternity of imperialist nations. But the Japanese were Asians, and therefore considered black sheep in a group dominated by Europeans. Much of Japan's reputation as a major power had come by way of its defeat of Czarist Russia in 1904–05. Yet at the same time, Japan was not quite the bogeyman it was made out to be. True Japan did have a powerful navy and a well-trained army. She had taken Korea and was satisfying her appetite for aggrandizement in Manchuria and China. But following her defeat of Czarist Russia, the financial strain of maintaining her position as a major power proved onerous. Theodore Roosevelt understood Tokyo's predicament. He was wise to such German machinations as a German-American-Chinese alliance against Japan. He saw through the "Yellow Peril" warnings that were being trumpeted in the Hearst newspapers. He also saw the danger in such oppressive measures taken by West Coast cities like San Francisco, which passed ordinances forbidding Japanese children from attending school. The Root-Takahira Agreement later helped to alleviate much of the tension that existed between Japan and the United States. But so did the subtle show of force. President Roosevelt's dispatch of the Atlantic Fleet Battleship Force to the Pacific served notice that the United States was serious about protecting its interests in the Philippines, Guam, and Hawaii.

Australia and New Zealand also shared American concerns about growing Japanese power. Like the United States, Australia had had incurred waves of Japanese immigration. But the feeling of unease in the Anzac nations was exacerbated by the retreat of the Royal Navy. This was due to the challenge posed by the rise of German naval power in the Atlantic—a challenge Britain could not afford to ignore. The United States Navy was seen by Wellington and Canberra, then, as a plausible counterweight to Japanese sea power. After all, the United States, Australia, and New Zealand shared an Anglo-Saxon heritage based on history, language, culture, and religion. At the same time, the Anzac nations would embark on naval expansion programs of their own. Yet one of the most significant aspects of the American fleet visit to the Land Down Under was the relationship that it spawned, a relationship that would later prove invaluable in two global conflicts.

Succeeding administrations in Washington did not forget the Pacific following the success of the Great White Fleet. The American presence in the Philippines was expanded and developed. Guam was turned into an important forward outpost. Work proceeded apace in developing Pearl Harbor into a major naval base. Regardless, the Atlantic was still considered the major theater of operations. Germany was viewed as the greatest threat and the kaiser as the globe's most dangerous personage. And while Roosevelt had correctly assessed the danger posed by surging German power, Teutonic ambitions were just part and parcel of the unquenchable greed inherent in the autocratic regimes of Europe. When the explosion occurred on June 28, 1914, in Sarajevo, the major naval clash when it came was in the North Sea in 1916 at a place called Jutland.

Jutland was the explosive culmination of the dreadnought race—a competition that saw many nations devote much of their time and treasure to build and stockpile the most powerful weapon in the early twentieth century. The battleship was the nuclear weapon of its day. Britain and Germany became the major competitors. By 1909, Germany had displaced the United States for the runner-up spot behind Britain's Royal Navy. Japan, France, Italy, and Russia were contenders, though not on as grand a scale as the Royal Navy and the High Seas Fleet. There were also regional powers vying for local hegemony, such as Austria-Hungary, Brazil, Argentina, and Chile.

The United States was a major player in the battleship-building competition. However, it is important to realize that the sailing of the Great White Fleet was not a contributing factor to the race; rather, it was an important event in it. President Roosevelt did not want war with Japan. Yet he was keen enough to understand the advantages of a peaceful demonstration of naval power, especially in light of the recent American inroads in the Pacific, and this from a nation that was beginning to emerge from its shell of introversion. For most of the nineteenth century, the major American pastime had been with expansion from coast to coast. This dynamism, known as Manifest Destiny, knew no bounds. And by 1898, this dynamism was like a bottle of carbonated liquid that had been shaken; it was ready to blow its top. And when it did, the soft drink known as America splashed all over the world.

The twentieth century would see American political, military, and economic power transform the world. The American cultural fabric would inexorably stitch itself onto the global textile of nations. By the conclusion of World War II, this never-before-seen transformation saw the United States emerge as a colossus on a war-torn globe. Unlike every other major combatant in World War II, the United States emerged with more food than it could eat, more clothes than it could wear, more gasoline than it could burn, and more money than it could spend. And it could all be directly attributed to the triumph of the Great White Fleet. If it can be said that Thomas Jefferson began the insatiable American desire to expand to the Pacific with the Louisiana Purchase, likewise it can be said the Theodore Roosevelt opened the American quest to become of global power with his fleet's historic circumnavigation of that globe. Indeed, the sailing of the Great White Fleet was the first major American strategic initiative in the twentieth century, and the first step on the road to making the twentieth century the American century.

It is quite easy to overlook the nuts-and-bolts aspects of an endeavor like the Great White Fleet when discussing the more prominent political, military, and strategic ramifications. For example, one of the most important reasons for the cruise was to see if it was possible to send a fleet halfway round the world and, upon its arrival, be in condition to battle a determined foe. The lesson of the debacle of the czarist fleet of 1904–05 was very much on the minds of navy planners in 1907. For it is important to remember that the warships of the early twentieth century, though marvels in their own right, were not as technologically and mechanically reliable as later types.

For instance, the cruise highlighted certain flaws in American battleship design. One such was the placement of armor belts. They did not extend far enough down the hull to provide protection against torpedo hits when the vessels rode high in a near-empty condition. Conversely, when the ships were heavily laden, the armor belts did not extend high enough to protect against incoming shells. These deficiencies were corrected in later battleship designs.

Another flaw was armament. The *Connecticut* class of pre-dreadnought mounted twelve seven-inch rifles in casemates along the hull. This caliber of projectile had been seen by the navy as the heaviest round that could be hand loaded and fired rapidly. But at 165 pounds per round, this proved not to be the case. And not only that, the seven-inchers were mounted too far down the hull to be of use in heavy seas. By 1917, the entire *Connecticut* class had their hull-mounted rifles removed and the casemates were plated over.

The issue of coal supplies has been touched on throughout the narrative. But its overriding importance to the success or failure of the Great White Fleet makes further scrutiny imperative. For an army or navy are only as good as its fuel supplies. For instance, during the battle of the Bulge, Hitler's panzers relied on captured American fuel dumps to maintain its advance. When this supply was denied, the advance came to an abrupt halt. The Great White Fleet sailed round the world, fueled for the most part by the British merchant marine. The lack of a viable homegrown merchant fleet and the insufficient number of naval auxiliaries was profoundly evident. True the United States had outposts in Samoa, the Philippines, Guam, and Hawaii. But these outposts were too few in number and not developed to the point of supporting a large fleet. A global net of coaling stations is what made the Royal Navy. British outposts were located in nearly every ocean and sea. The British merchant marine was the world's largest and carried the most tonnage of every shippable commodity, including coal. It was clearly obvious that in case of a conflict in some far-flung corner of the globe, the United States Navy stood a good chance of being left high and dry.

At the conclusion of the round-the-world cruise, an attempt was made to rectify the situation. Five new colliers were laid down in American yards. These were in addition to the pair already under construction. The collier, unlike a stationary land base, provided mobility and, in theory, was less likely to fall prey to enemy attack. With enough auxiliaries and a large merchant marine, it would be possible for the fleet to maintain itself almost indefinitely. For the United States Navy, any semblance of this did not appear until the advent of liquid fuels. At the time of the round-the-world cruise, coal was still the fuel of choice of the world's navies. Oil was first tried in 1867. It was cleaner and easier to handle. But supplies of oil were scarce and, in comparison to coal, cost prohibitive.

But like every other industry touched by the Industrial Revolution, the technology was soon developed to unlock the earth's treasure trove of petroleum. In 1909, the United States Navy began the conversion to oil-fired power plants. By the following year, all new submarines and destroyers burned oil. The battleships *North Carolina* and *Florida* were the first hybrid capital ships in the U.S. Navy, burning both oil and coal. It was the *Nevada,* launched in 1914, that was the first American battleship to be powered solely by oil.

But the ability of the fleet to sustain itself was not possible until World War II. At the onset of the conflict, the demands on American shipyards to construct a two-ocean navy and merchant marine seemed overwhelming. In the Atlantic, Doenitz's U-boats were taking such a toll of allied shipping that it seemed only a matter of time before the Atlantic lifeline would be cut and Britain would be starved into submission. Yet American shipyards and industry were galvanized for the daunting task at hand. The allies went from losing ships faster than they were being built to building ships faster than they were sunk. In a mind-boggling display of production, keels were laid by the thousands. There were transports and freighters to carry troops, tanks, and guns; tankers to carry an unending supply of gasoline and oil; and the indispensable escorts to protect them. Destroyers, corvettes, sloops, and baby flat-tops, all equipped with the latest weaponry and electronic aids, went on to defeat the underwater menace and secure the Atlantic lifeline.

In the Pacific, superior American production turned

out aircraft carriers in quantity and quality for the navy's counterattack following the debacle at Pearl Harbor. The remarkable *Essex*-class fleet carrier formed the backbone of the most superlative naval strike force in history. More than two dozen of these vessels were built, together with the new generation of fast battleships, cruisers, and destroyers, which utterly overwhelmed the Imperial Navy at the Philippine Sea and Leyte Gulf. This fleet could remain at sea almost indefinitely. A support fleet of oilers, transports, and escorts kept the fast carrier task forces fueled and supplied for extended periods in distant waters. This is one of the enduring legacies of the Great White Fleet—long legs for cruising and a method of resupply that was massive and mobile. These lessons learned from the round-the-world cruise proved invaluable in winning the war at sea during World War II.

The men and ships of the Great White Fleet accomplished a feat of monumental historical significance. Circumnavigating the globe with coal-burners to the tune of forty-six thousand miles was an accomplishment in itself. Yet it is important to remember that even though the fleet succeeded in impressing the world, every ship was virtually obsolete when it departed Hampton Roads on December 16, 1907.

The composition of the Great White Fleet was made up of the pre-dreadnought type of battleship. Typical tonnage ranged from 14,000 to 17,650. Main armament was a hodgepodge of calibers. Generally, it consisted of four twelve-inch supported by five-inch, six-inch, seven-inch, or eight-inch guns. The basic idea behind such an array of armament was simple: Bash your opponent with the twelve-inch guns while an array of medium calibers raked the bridge, fire control, light gun positions, and exposed personnel. Yet improvements in ordnance and fire control extended the range of engagement. This rendered light and medium calibers noticeably less effective at extended ranges. Add to this the fact that torpedo ranges were increasing as well.

Advancements in gunnery spurred the appropriate improvements in ship design. In 1903, Vittorio Cuniberti, the chief constructor of the Italian Navy, published an article in the annual edition of *Jane's Fighting Ships*, advocating the "all big gun" battleship. He broached the idea of a new generation of battleship with a single major caliber of armament with the Italian Navy, but was rebuffed. Meanwhile, the United States was already moving in that direction. The navy presented an appropriation request to Congress in the spring of 1904 for a dreadnought. Funds were made available the following year. However, it was not until December 1906 that the *South Carolina* and the *Michigan* were laid down. Both vessels would mount eight twelve-inch guns, displace 17,617 tons, and have a top speed of 18.5 knots.

In Britain, the redoubtable Jackie Fisher wrote in his memoirs that he had conceived of the idea of a single major caliber ship back in 1900. When he became First Sea Lord on 1904, he put his theory into practice. HMS *Dreadnought* was laid down in Portsmouth on October 2, 1905. In an astounding display of production, the battleship was launched on February 10, 1906. She was completed just eight months later on October 3. *Dreadnought* revolutionized battleship design overnight. She displaced

21,845 tons at full load. Her steam turbines could drive her to a top speed of twenty-one knots. And, more importantly, she mounted ten twelve-inch guns. Here was a battleship that could not only outrun any pre-dreadnought in existence, but engage two of them at the same time.

Yet despite the fact that the ships of the Great White Fleet were obsolete at the time of sailing, what they accomplished on their history-making cruise has been, for the most part, largely understated. That the cruise helped to elevate the United States to the ranks of the global powers has already been discussed, but what it did for the United States Navy is beyond question. It did, without a doubt, sell the navy to the public. Many Americans avidly followed the exploits of the fleet through newspaper accounts and magazine stories. It also raised in Americans an awareness of international affairs.

It is not an injudicious thing to say that since the sailing of the Great White Fleet, the United States has maintained its commitment to sea power. For without control of the seas, a global power has less chance of controlling its destiny. This fact has never been more relevant than today. With the United States importing half of all the oil it requires, keeping the sea lanes open is not only vital, but literally a matter of life and death. No other service but the navy can perform this function. If any lesson at all can be discerned from the cruise of the Great White Fleet, it is that any potential adversary must be made to know that it is not beyond the global reach of the United States Navy. But just as the navy can use its long-range striking power in defense of American strategic interests, it can also be used to render the most humanitarian of assistance. Witness the aftermath of the catastrophic tsunami that struck Southeast Asia in 2004. Just like the assistance rendered by units of the Great White Fleet to hard-pressed Italians in the aftermath of the disastrous earthquake in 1909, warships and aircraft of the United States Navy joined in relief efforts to those in Indonesia and other countries that had been savaged by nature's wrath.

Yet perhaps the greatest legacy of the Great White Fleet was the impression of America that it cast upon the world. As was seen throughout the narrative, many of the nations along the route received the globetrotters with exuberant fanfare and genuine hospitality. It was, to be sure, a much-simpler time; a romantic era where the semblance of chivalry still existed and life was not the cold, complicated thing that human beings have made it out to be in the hundred years hence. It was an era before the tragedy of two global conflicts caused the extermination of some 70 million souls. It was an era before the advent of nuclear weapons and the threat of global Armageddon. It was an era of a Yankee dynamism that burst upon the world scene with an insatiable quest for new markets and inventions. A dynamism guided in no small part by the lure of profits as expected to be garnered by the American capitalist of the time, but a dynamism that lacked the cynicism prevalent in today's crop of America's royalty. A cynicism based on a fear of the transient nature of America's status as a global power; an era where American power is based no longer on a concrete foundation of confidence, community, and credit, but on a sandy base of discord, doubt, and debt. To think the United States could have continued its post-World War II economic, political, and military dominance for an indefinite period of time was not only short-sighted but incredibly absurd. The post-war resurgence of Europe and the post-colonial maturation of such nations as India and China are indicative of the changing nature of power; a permutation of economic and political realities with which the United States seems hardly able to cope.

Vietnam starkly manifested the limits of American military and political power. Japan showed itself to be a bona fide economic competitor, bringing to an end American dominance in such industries as automobiles and electronics. Threats to foreign sources of oil in 1973, 1979, and 1990 laid bare America's energy vulnerability. Such is the cost of the indolent pace of pursuit of alternative sources of energy; a lethargy spurred on by the gluttonous consumption of a spoiled consumer and the avarice of the special interests addicted to today's profits versus investing in tomorrow's energy independence.

In ten short decades, Manifest Destiny has evolved into Evident Fatalism. The willingness of the contemporary generation to mortgage America's future economic vitality with a calamitous burden of debt heralds the demise of American society, economy, and political freedom as we know it. Nowhere is this mirrored any clearer than in the Bush Administration's prostitution of the War on Terror by propagating the costly fiction of bringing democracy to a nation like Iraq. This patchwork quilt of conflicting ethnicity, clannish traditions, tribal affiliations, and religious fervor has little or no chance of grasping the concept of freedom of expression and representative government as practiced in the West. At the same time Washington sells this bill-of-goods to the electorate, it imperils freedom of expression at home in the dubious pursuit of security. If, one hundred years later, the United States Navy wished to commemorate the accomplishment of the Great White Fleet with another circumnavigation of the globe, it would indeed be interesting to see how many of the nations along the original route would find America appealing enough to welcome the fleet to their shores.

TABLE ONE[1]

DISPOSITION OF THE GREAT WHITE FLEET: HAMPTON ROADS TO SAN FRANCISCO

Flag Commander: Rear Admiral Robley D. Evans*

Fleet Flagship: USS *Connecticut* (BB-18)

First Battleship Squadron: Rear Admiral Robley D. Evans

First Battleship Division	Second Battleship Division
Rear Admiral Robley D. Evans:	Rear Admiral William H. Emory:
USS *Connecticut* (BB-18) Captain Hugo Osterhaus	USS *Georgia* (BB-15) Captain Henry McCrea
USS *Kansas* (BB-21) Captain Charles E. Vreeland	USS *New Jersey* (BB-16) Captain William Southerland
USS *Vermont* (BB-20) Captain William P. Potter	USS *Rhode Island* (BB-17) Captain Joseph B. Murdock
USS *Louisiana* (BB-19) Captain Richard Wainwright	USS *Virginia* (BB-13) Captain Seaton Schroeder

Second Battleship Squadron:
Rear Admiral Charles M. Thomas

Third Battleship Division	Fourth Battleship Division
Rear Admiral Charles M. Thomas:	Rear Admiral Charles S. Sperry:
USS *Minnesota* (BB-22) Captain John Hubbard	USS *Alabama* (BB-08)** Captain Ten Eyck DeW Veeder

USS *Ohio* (BB-12)
Captain Charles W. Bartlett

USS *Illinois* (BB-07)
Captain John M. Bowyer

USS *Missouri* (BB-11)
Captain Greenlief A. Merriam

USS *Kearsarge* (BB-05)
Captain Hamilton Hutchins

USS *Maine* (BB-10)**
Captain Giles B. Harber

USS *Kentucky* (BB-06)
Captain Walter C. Cowles

Accompanying Fleet Auxiliaries

USS *Yankton* (tender)
Lieutenant Walter R. Gherardi

USS *Culgoa* (store ship)
Lt. Commander John B. Patton

USS *Glacier* (store ship)
Commander William S. Hogg

USS *Relief* (hospital ship)

USS *Panther* (repair ship)
Commander Valentine S. Nelson

Destroyer Escort, "Torpedo-Boat Flotilla"

USS *Whipple*
Lt. Hutchinson I. Cone

USS *Hopkins*
Lt. Alfred G. Howe

USS *Arethusa* (tender)
Commander Albert Grant

USS *Truxton*
Lt. Charles S. Kerrick

USS *Hull*
Lt. Frank McCommon

USS *Stewart*
Lt. Julius F. Hellwig

USS *Lawrence*
Lt. Ernest Frederick

*Rear Admiral Evans was in ill health at the start of the voyage. His condition deteriorated as the cruise progressed. Admiral Evans was detached from *Connecticut* on April 1, 1908, and officially relieved from duty on May 9. Rear Admiral Charles

M. Thomas assumed command, but only for six days. Thomas was due for retirement in October, and he was plagued with a heart condition. Admiral Thomas died less than two months later from a heart attack. Rear Admiral Charles S. Sperry transferred his flag to *Connecticut* on May 15, 1908, as the third and final commander of the Great White Fleet. Rear Admiral William H. Emory assumed command of Second Battleship Squadron. The resulting vacancies were filled by Captain Seaton Schroeder of *Virginia* and Captain Richard Wainwright of *Louisiana*. Both men were elevated to flag rank.

**Prior to the Great White Fleet's departure from San Francisco for the Pacific leg of the voyage, battleships *Maine* and *Alabama* were replaced by *Nebraska* and *Wisconsin*. *Maine* was replaced due to a voracious appetite for coal. *Alabama* was sidelined for a cracked cylinder head.

DISPOSITION OF THE GREAT WHITE FLEET: SAN FRANCISCO TO MANILA BAY

Flag Commander: Rear Admiral Charles S. Sperry

Fleet Flagship: USS *Connecticut* (BB-18)

First Battleship Squadron: Rear Admiral Charles S. Sperry

First Battleship Division	Second Battleship Division
Rear Admiral Charles S. Sperry:	Rear Admiral Richard Wainwright:
USS *Connecticut* (BB-18) Captain Hugo Osterhaus	USS *Georgia* (BB-15) Captain Edward F. Qualtrough
USS *Kansas* (BB-21) Captain Charles E. Vreeland	USS *Nebraska* (BB-14)* Captain Reginald F. Nicholson
USS *Minnesota* (BB-22) Captain John Hubbard	USS *New Jersey* (BB-16) Captain William Southerland
USS *Vermont* (BB-20) Captain William P. Potter	USS *Rhode Island* (BB-17) Captain Joseph B. Murdock

Second Battleship Squadron:
Rear Admiral William H. Emory

Third Battleship Division	Fourth Battleship Division
Rear Admiral William H. Emory:	Rear Admiral Seaton Schroeder:
USS *Louisiana* (BB-19)	USS *Wisconsin* (BB-09)
Captain Kossuth Niles*	Captain Frank E. Beatty*
USS *Virginia* (BB-13)	USS *Illinois* (BB-07)*
Captain Alexander Sharp*	Captain John M. Bowyer
USS *Missouri* (BB-11)	USS *Kearsarge* (BB-05)
Captain Robert M. Doyle	Captain Hamilton Hutchins
USS *Ohio* (BB-12)	USS *Kentucky* (BB-06)
Captain Thomas B. Howard	Captain Joseph B. Murdock

Accompanying Fleet Auxiliaries

USS *Yankton* (tender)	USS *Culgoa* (store ship)
Lt. Commander Charles B. McVay	Lt. Commander John B. Patton
USS *Glacier* (store ship)	USS *Relief* (hospital ship)
Commander William S. Hogg	Surgeon Charles F. Stokes
USS *Panther* (repair ship)	
Commander Valentine S. Nelson	

*The batting order of the fleet was altered somewhat. *Minnesota* was sent to First Division. *Louisiana* was made Admiral Emory's flagship, making it flagship of Second Squadron and Third Division. With the removal of *Alabama* for a cracked cylinder head, *Wisconsin* assumed flagship position of Fourth Division, flying the flag of Rear Admiral Seaton Schroeder. Newly arrived *Nebraska* was assigned to Second Division, sending *Virginia* to Third Division. Captain Alexander Sharp took over as skipper of *Virginia* when Captain Seaton Schroeder was promoted to flag rank and given to command Fourth Division from *Wisconsin*. Captain Richard Wainwright relinquished *Louisiana* when he was promoted to flag rank and assigned to command Second Division from aboard *Georgia*.

DISPOSITION OF THE GREAT WHITE FLEET: MANILA BAY TO HAMPTON ROADS

Flag Commander: Rear Admiral Charles S. Sperry

Fleet Flagship: USS *Connecticut* (BB-18)

First Battleship Squadron: Rear Admiral Charles S. Sperry

First Battleship Division	Second Battleship Division
Rear Admiral Charles S. Sperry:	Rear Admiral Richard Wainwright:
USS *Connecticut* (BB-18)	USS *Georgia* (BB-15)
Captain Hugo Osterhaus	Captain Edward F. Qualtrough*
USS *Vermont* (BB-20)	USS *Nebraska* (BB-14)
Captain Frank F. Fletcher**	Captain Reginald F. Nicholson
USS *Kansas* (BB-21)	USS *New Jersey* (BB-16)
Captain Charles E. Vreeland	Captain William Southerland
USS *Minnesota* (BB-22)	USS *Rhode Island* (BB-17)
Captain John Hubbard	Captain Joseph B. Murdock

Second Battleship Squadron: Rear Admiral Seaton Schroeder

Third Battleship Division	Fourth Battleship Division
Rear Admiral Seaton Schroeder:	Rear Admiral William P. Potter:**
USS *Louisiana* (BB-19)	USS *Wisconsin* (BB-09)
Captain Kossuth Niles	Captain Frank E. Beatty
USS *Virginia* (BB-13)	USS *Illinois* (BB-07)
Captain Alexander Sharp	Captain John M. Bowyer
USS *Missouri* (BB-11)	USS *Kearsarge* (BB-05)
Captain Robert M. Doyle	Captain Hamilton Hutchins
USS *Ohio* (BB-12)	USS *Kentucky* (BB-06)
Captain Thomas B. Howard	Captain Walter C. Cowles

Accompanying Fleet Auxiliaries

USS *Yankton* (tender)	USS *Panther* (repair ship)
Lt. Commander Charles B. McVay	Commander Valentine S. Nelson
USS *Culgoa* (store ship)	
Lt. Commander John B. Patton	

*Captain Edward F. Qualtrough was removed as commander of USS *Georgia* when the fleet reached Gibraltar. He was accused of drunkenness when his ship was in Tangier. While the court-martial board ruled in the skipper's favor, Rear Admiral Sperry did not and had him relieved of command. Captain Qualtrough was replaced by Lieutenant-Commander George C. Kline.

**After Second Battleship Squadron left Amoy to rejoin First Battleship Squadron in the Philippines, Second Squadron flagship *Louisiana* detached and headed for Hong Kong. Rear Admiral William H. Emory disembarked at the British colony for the trip home and retirement. *Louisiana* rejoined the fleet at Manila Bay. Rear Admiral Seaton Schroeder was promoted to commander of Second Battleship Squadron and commander of Third Battleship Division. His place as commander of Fourth Division was filled by Rear Admiral William P. Potter. Potter's place as skipper of USS *Vermont* was filled by Captain Frank E. Fletcher.

TABLE TWO

BATTLESHIPS OF THE GREAT WHITE FLEET: CONNECTICUT CLASS

Five* of the sixteen battleships in the Great White Fleet were from the *Connecticut* class. At the time, the *Connecticuts* were the latest and best pre-dreadnought battleships America had to offer. The *Connecticuts* were the largest single class of battleship ever produced by the United States.

USS *Connecticut* (BB-18)   Captain Hugo Osterhaus

USS *Louisiana* (BB-19)   Captain Richard Wainwright**

USS *Vermont* (BB-20)   Captain William P. Potter***

USS *Kansas* (BB-21)   Captain Charles E. Vreeland

USS *Minnesota* (BB-22)   Captain John H. Hubbard

Standard Displacement: 16,000 tons

Full Load Displacement: 17,650 tons

Overall Length: 456' 4"

Beam: 76' 10"

Draught: 24' 6"

Complement: 827 officers and men, 916 as a flagship

Protection: Maximum armor, 12", turret face plates

Maximum Shaft Horsepower: 16,500

Fuel: Coal

Maximum Speed: 18 knots

Powerplant: Vertical triple expansion type, four cylinders, reciprocating. Babcock and Wilcox boilers. Two screws.

Main Armament: Four 12-inch 45 caliber; eight 8-inch 45 caliber; twelve 7-inch 45 caliber.

Secondary Armament: Twenty 3-inch 50 caliber; twelve 3-pounder; four 1-pounder; four .30 caliber machine guns.

Torpedo Tubes: Four 21-inch submerged type.

*The sixth ship of the *Connecticut* class, USS *New Hampshire* (BB-25), was not commissioned until March 19, 1908, too late to join her sisters for the round-the-world cruise. However, BB-25 was part of Rear Admiral Conway H. Arnold's escort force that met the returning Great White Fleet in the Atlantic on February 17, 1909, and entered Hampton Roads five days later as part of Admiral Sperry's task force.

**Captain Richard Wainwright began the round-the-world cruise as commander of USS *Louisiana.* With Rear Admiral Charles S. Sperry assuming overall command of the Great White Fleet in San Francisco, Captain Richard Wainwright became Rear Admiral Richard Wainwright in command of Second Battleship Division. Captain Kossuth Niles took over as skipper of USS *Louisiana,* a command post he held for the rest of the voyage.

***Captain William P. Potter began the round-the-world cruise as commander of USS *Vermont* (BB-20). Potter held this command until the fleet reached Manila Bay. With the retirement of Rear Admiral William H. Emory, Rear Admiral Seaton Schroeder assumed command of Second

Battleship Squadron. Potter was promoted to flag rank and assumed command of Fourth Battleship Division. Captain Frank F. Fletcher took over as skipper of USS *Vermont*.

VIRGINIA CLASS

Four* of the original sixteen battleships of the Great White Fleet were from the *Virginia* class of pre-dreadnought battleships. They were as follows:

USS *Virginia* (BB-13)	Captain Seaton Schroeder**
USS *Georgia* (BB-15)	Captain Henry McCray
USS *New Jersey* (BB-16)	Captain William Southerland
USS *Rhode Island* (BB-17)	Captain Joseph B. Murdock
Standard Displacement: 14,948 tons	Protection: Maximum armor, 12", turret face plates
Full Load Displacement: 16,094 tons	Maximum Shaft Horsepower: 16,500
Overall Length: 441' 3"	Fuel: Coal
Beam: 76' 3"	Maximum Speed: 18 knots
Draught: 23' 9"	Complement: 812 officers and men

Powerplant: Vertical inverted triple expansion type, four cylinders, reciprocating. Babcock and Wilcox boilers. Two screws.

Main Armament: Four 12-inch 45 caliber; eight 8-inch 45 caliber; twelve 6-inch 50 caliber.

Secondary Armament: Twelve 3-inch 50 caliber; twelve 3-pounder; eight .30 caliber machine guns.

Torpedo Tubes: Four 21-inch submerged type.

Virginia-class battleship, USS *Nebraska* (BB-14), joined the fleet in San Francisco. BB-14 replaced USS *Maine* (BB-10), removed from the line up because of excessive fuel consumption.

**Captain Seaton Schroeder began the cruise in command of USS *Virginia* (BB-13). While the fleet was in San Francisco, Captain Schroeder was promoted to rear admiral and given command of Fourth Battleship Division, following Admiral Sperry's promotion to task force commander. Captain Alexander Sharp assumed command of USS *Virginia*.

MAINE CLASS

The entire class of *Maine* pre-dreadnought battleships began the round-the-world cruise.
They are listed as follows:

USS *Maine* (BB10)*

USS *Missouri* (BB-11)

USS *Ohio* (BB-12)

Standard Displacement: 12,846 tons

Full Load Displacement: 13,500 tons

Overall Length: 393' 11"

Beam: 72' 3"

Draught: 24' 4"

Complement: 561 officers and men

Captain Giles B. Harber

Captain Greenlief A. Merriam

Captain Charles W. Bartlett

Protection: Maximum armor: 12", turret face plates

Maximum Shaft Horsepower: 16,000

Fuel: Coal

Maximum Speed: 18 knots

Powerplant: Vertical inverted triple expansion type, four cylinders, reciprocating. Babcock and Wilcox boilers. Two screws.

Main Armament: Four 12-inch 45 caliber; sixteen 6-inch 50 caliber.

Secondary Armament: Six 3-inch 50 caliber; eight 3-pounder; six 1-pounder; three .30 caliber machine guns.

Torpedo Tubes: Two 18-inch submerged type.

*USS *Maine* (BB10) was dropped from the Great White Fleet at San Francisco. The reason was the ship's excessive appetite for coal. USS *Nebraska* (BB-14) continued the round-the-world cruise as *Maine's* replacement. The inclusion of *Nebraska* meant that the entire *Virginia* class was represented.

ILLINOIS CLASS

Two vessels represented the *Illinois* class of pre-dreadnought when the Great White Fleet departed Hampton Roads on December 16, 1907. The pair is listed below:

USS *Illinois* (BB-07)

USS *Alabama* (BB-08)*

Standard Displacement: 11,565 tons

Full Load Displacement: 12,150 tons

Maximum Shaft Horsepower: 10,000

Draught: 23' 4"

Complement: 536 officers and men

Captain John M. Bowyer

Captain Ten Eyck DeW Veeder

Protection: Maximum armor: 16.5", turret face plates

Overall Length: 375' 4"

Beam: 72' 3" Fuel: Coal

Maximum Speed: 16 knots

Powerplant: Vertical inverted triple expansion type, three cylinders, reciprocating. Newport News type, FT no. 8 boilers.

Main Armament: Four 13-inch 35 caliber; fourteen 6-inch 40 caliber.

Secondary Armament: Sixteen 6-pounder; six 1-pounder; four .30 caliber machine guns.

Torpedo Tubes: Four 18-inch surface type.

*USS *Alabama* (BB-08) was replaced at San Francisco by

her sister USS *Wisconsin* (BB-09). The former was side-lined due to a cracked cylinder head. With the insertion of *Wisconsin* into the batting order, the *Illinois* class was still represented by two vessels.

KEARSARGE CLASS

The entire *Kearsarge* class of two pre-dreadnoughts began and finished the round-the-world cruise. The *Kearsarges* were the oldest vessels in the Great White Fleet.

USS *Kearsarge* (BB-05)*
USS *Kentucky* (BB-06)
Standard Displacement: 11,540 tons

Full Load Displacement: 12,320 tons
Maximum Shaft Horsepower: 10,000
Draught: 23' 6"
Complement: 554 officers and men

Captain Hamilton Hutchins
Captain Walter C. Cowles
Protection: Maximum armor: 17", turret face plates
Overall Length: 375' 4"
Beam: 72' 3" Fuel: Coal
Maximum Speed: 16 knots

Powerplant: Vertical inverted triple expansion type, three cylinders, reciprocating. Newport News, FT no. 5 boilers.

Main Armament: Four 13-inch 35 caliber; four 8-inch 35 caliber; fourteen 5-inch 40 caliber.

Secondary Armament: Twenty 6-pounder; eight 1-pounder; four .30 caliber machine guns.

Torpedo Tubes: Four 18-inch surface type.

*It used to be that warships of the United States Navy were named in certain fashion depending on ship type. For instance, battleships were named after states, cruisers for cities, destroyers for famous people, and submarines for fish. There was just one battleship in the history of the United States Navy that was not named for a state. That was USS *Kearsarge* (BB-05). *Kearsarge* was so named by Act of Congress in commemoration of the famed Civil War sloop that ended the predatory career of the Confederate raider CSS *Alabama*. However, it is interesting to note that the only American battleship not named for a state would go on to enjoy the longest term of uninterrupted service of any American battleship.

Kearsarge was launched March 24, 1898, and commissioned on February 20, 1900. Sponsor was Mrs. Herbert Winslow, daughter-in-law of Captain John Winslow, who commanded the Civil War *Kearsarge* at the time of her famous engagement with *Alabama*.

Kearsarge served as flagship for the North Atlantic Fleet. She was flagship of the European Squadron in 1903, when the American force visited the continent. On December 16, 1907, BB-05 was part of the famed Great White Fleet and steamed more than 46,000 miles in circumnavigation of the globe. *Kearsarge* took part in American actions off Vera Cruz in 1915 and 1916. When America joined World War I, BB-05 was used as a platform to train gunners for action in the Atlantic. On August 18, 1918, while off Boston, *Kearsarge* rescued twenty-six Norwegian seamen after their ship had been sunk by U-117.

Following World War I, *Kearsarge*, as an engineering

training ship, made a final midshipman sortie in May 1919. Then on May 10, 1920, *Kearsarge* was decommissioned as a battleship and was designated AB-1. *Kearsarge* traded her armament for a huge crane. Her hull was modified with blisters for increased stability as a crane ship. Her most notable accomplishment in her second career was in the salvage of the submarine *Squalus* off the coast of New Hampshire in 1939.

On November 6, 1941, AB-1 was renamed *Crane Ship No. 1*. The name *Kearsarge* was designated for a new *Essex*-class carrier CV-12. This was changed, too, when CV-12 was renamed *Hornet* in honor of CV-07 lost to enemy action off Santa Cruz on October 27, 1942. The name *Kearsarge* was later applied to CV-33.

Crane Ship No. 1 performed her duty faithfully in hoisting turrets, superstructures, and armor in the construction of numerous warships during World War II. Following the war, she was used in the Boston Navy Yard until she had outlived her usefulness. She was finally decommissioned on June 22, 1955, and was sold for scrap on August 9, 1955, after fifty-five years of continuous service.

CHRONOLOGY OF THE GREAT WHITE FLEET

HAMPTON ROADS TO SAN FRANCISCO

1907

December 16.   The Great White Fleet departs Hampton Roads for San Francisco.

December 20.   Fleet is off Puerto Rico. *Kentucky* and *Illinois* drop out due to engineering problems. Both make repairs quickly. The former rejoins the fleet. The latter puts into Culebra to drop off a seaman who was taken sick. *Missouri* heads for San Juan to put ashore another seaman who fell ill.

December 21.   *Illinois* and *Missouri* rejoin the fleet.

December 22.   Ordinary seaman Robert Eugenpipes dies. The *Alabama* seaman's body is committed to the deep in the Caribbean Sea.

December 23. The Great White Fleet arrives at Port-of-Spain. The British colony is the first port-of-call on the cruise.

December 29. The fleet departs Port-of-Spain bound for Rio de Janeiro.

1908

January 12. The Great White Fleet arrives at Rio de Janeiro.

January 22. The fleet departs Rio de Janeiro.

January 22. On board *Ohio*, seaman Frank Tew dies. His body is committed to the deep in the South Atlantic.

January 26. The fleet rendezvoused with the Argentine San Martin Division, featuring the cruisers *San Martin, Buenos Ayres, Pueyrredon*, and *9 de Julio*.

January 27. The San Martin Division breaks off and heads for home. The Great White Fleet continues south for the tip of South America.

January 31. The Great White Fleet arrives at Possession Bay, gateway to the Strait of Magellan.

February 1.	The fleet arrives at Punta Arenas in the Strait of Magellan.
February 7.	The fleet departs Punta Arenas.
February 8.	The fleet transits the Strait of Magellan and enters the Pacific Ocean.
February 14.	The fleet performs a sail-by at Valparaiso.
February 19.	The Peruvian cruiser *Bolognesi* joins the Great White Fleet as an escort.
February 20.	The Great White Fleet anchors at Callao to begin the visit to Peru.
February 29.	The fleet departs Callao and heads for Magdalena Bay, Mexico.
March 12.	The fleet arrives at Magdalena Bay. The battleships will remain here for the next several weeks engaged in range calibration exercises and target practice.
March 30.	USS *Connecticut* leaves Magdalena Bay, lifts Admiral Robley D. Evans to California for hospitalization in Paso Robles.
April 4.	USS *Connecticut* returns to Magdalena Bay. Rear Admiral Charles M. Thomas unfurls his flag as the new task force commander. Rear Admiral Charles S. Sperry moves up as deputy commander.

April 11.	The fleet leaves Magdalena Bay, heading north for California.
April 14.	The fleet reaches San Diego.
April 18.	The fleet visits San Pedro.
April 19.	First Battleship Division remains at San Pedro. Second Division pushes on for Long Beach; Third Division heads for Santa Monica; and Fourth Division to Redondo Beach.
April 25.	The fleet reassembles for the short steam to Santa Barbara.
April 30.	The fleet departs Santa Barbara for Monterey, arrives May 1.
May 2.	Rear Admiral Robley D. Evans journeys up from Paso Robles and is piped aboard the *Connecticut*. The ailing commander-in-chief will lead the fleet one more time for its triumphal entry into San Francisco. First Battleship Squadron heads for Santa Cruz.
May 4.	Second Battleship Squadron links up with First Squadron. The torpedo-boat flotilla joins the fleet at Santa Cruz.
May 5.	The fleet anchors for the night off the Golden Gate. Battleships *Nebraska* and *Wisconsin* and the armored cruisers of the Pacific Fleet join up.

May 6.	Forty-two warships and auxiliaries, the largest concentration of naval might ever gathered in the Western Hemisphere up to that time, makes its entrance into San Francisco Bay.
May 7.	Grand parade through the streets of San Francisco. 7,500 sailors and marines, the largest naval force ever landed in peacetime or in war up to that time, comes ashore. At the head of the procession, occupying a carriage with the mayor is the ailing Rear Admiral Robley D. Evans.
May 8.	Secretary of the Navy Victor H. Metcalf reviews the fleet.
May 9.	Rear Admiral Robley D. Evans retires. Rear Admiral Charles M. Thomas assumes honorary command of the Great White Fleet.
May 15.	Rear Admiral Charles Stillman Sperry officially takes command of the Great White Fleet. He is the third and final commander of the round-the-world cruise.
May 18.	*Maine* and *Alabama* are replaced by *Nebraska* and *Wisconsin*. The fleet leaves San Francisco bound for the Pacific Northwest.

May 21.	The fleet steams into Puget Sound for Seattle.
May 23.	First and Third Divisions depart for San Francisco. Second Division visits Bremerton while Fourth Division heads for Tacoma.
May 27.	Second and Fourth Divisions head for San Francisco. First and Third Divisions begin refits for the Pacific leg of the cruise.
June 25.	The fleet's route of return is officially announced. The fleet will return to Hampton Roads via the Pacific, Mediterranean, and Atlantic. Arrival date is set for February 22, 1909, George Washington's birthday.
July 3.	Del Monte, California. Rear Admiral Charles M. Thomas dies of a heart attack.

SAN FRANCISCO TO
HAMPTON ROADS

July 7.　　　The Great White Fleet departs San Francisco for Hawaii. *Nebraska* is left behind due to an outbreak of scarlet fever.

July 9.　　　Health officials declare *Nebraska* fit for departure. The battleship rejoins the fleet at sea on July 14.

July 16.　　　Fleet arrives at Honolulu.

July 22.　　　The fleet leaves Hawaii for New Zealand. *Minnesota* is left behind to collect the mail.

July 28.　　　*Minnesota* rejoins the fleet.

August 2.　　　Fleet conducts sail-by of American Samoa.

August 9.　　　The Great White Fleet visits Auckland.

August 14.　　　Sperry's task force leaves New Zealand.

August 18.　　　Fleet rides out a two-day storm in the Tasman Sea. Damage is minimal and no men are lost.

August 20.	The fleet calls on Sydney.
August 23.	Sailors and marines join Royal Navy and Commonwealth armed forces personnel in a grand military review. At 12,000 strong, it is the largest review of its kind ever held in Australia up to that time.
August 27.	The fleet departs Sydney.
August 29.	The fleet calls on Melbourne.
September 6.	The fleet departs Melbourne. Kansas is left behind to collect the mail and round up deserters.
September 15.	*Kansas* rejoins the fleet at Albany. Aboard are 458 bags of mail and more than 100 deserters. More than 100 strays are still at large in Melbourne. With a schedule to keep, these men are left behind.
September 18.	The fleet departs Albany. *Missouri* and *Connecticut* delayed due to refueling.
September 26.	The fleet enters the Java Sea via the Lombok Strait.
September 30.	The fleet sails by Zamboanga on Mindanao.
October 2.	The fleet reaches Manila Bay. Due to a cholera epidemic, crews are restricted to their ships. Fleet takes on fuel.
October 10.	The fleet departs Manila Bay for Japan.

October 12.	The runs fleet into a typhoon. Several ships incur minor damage. Three seaman from *Rhode Island* are swept overboard. Two are rescued, but gunner's mate William Fuller is lost.
October 18.	The Great White Fleet reaches Yokohama.
October 19.	This day is proclaimed American Day in Tokyo.
October 20.	Admiral Sperry, his flag officers, and battleship skippers attend a luncheon as guests of the emperor.
October 25.	The fleet departs Japan.
October 27.	The fleet splits up. First Battleship Squadron continues on to the Philippines. Second Battleship Squadron heads for Amoy, China.
October 30.	Second Squadron arrives at Amoy.
November 5.	Second Squadron departs Amoy. *Louisiana* detaches and heads for Hong Kong to deposit Rear Admiral Emory, who heads home to begin retirement.
November 7.	Second Battleship Squadron arrives at Manila Bay. *Louisiana* follows two days later.

December 1.   The Great White Fleet departs Manila
                 Bay.

December 6.   The fleet performs a sail-by at Singapore.
                 The American battleships enter the Strait
                 of Malacca.

December 9.   The fleet breaks into the Andaman Sea.
                 Georgia is released and sent ahead to
                 Colombo because a case of small pox is
                 diagnosed. Rest of the crew who went
                 ashore at Manila is inoculated.

December 13.   Rest of the Great White Fleet joins
                 Georgia at Ceylon.

December 20.   The fleet departs Ceylon.

December 26.   The fleet reaches the island of Socotra.

December 27.   The fleet enters the Gulf of Aden, heads
                 for the Red Sea.

1909

January 3.   The Great White Fleet reaches the Suez
                 Canal.

January 4–7.   Fleet transits the Suez Canal in three
                 groups, bound for Port Said and
                 refueling.

January 5.   Flagship *Connecticut* heads for Messina
                 to assist with relief efforts following the

earthquake and tidal wave that devastates southern Italy. *Vermont*, *Kansas*, and *Minnesota* steam for Villefranche, France.

January 6.   *Louisiana* and *Virginia* leave Port Said for Smyrna.

January 8.   *Georgia* and *Nebraska* leave Port Said and head for Marseilles. *Kentucky* heads for Tripoli. *Ohio* and *Missouri* steam for Athens.

January 9.   *Connecticut* arrives in disaster-wracked Messina. *New Jersey* and *Rhode Island* leave Port Said for Marseilles.

January 10.   *Illinois, Kearsarge,* and *Wisconsin* depart Port Said for Malta.

January 11.   *Illinois* rerouted to Messina to assist in disaster clean up. Rejoins sisters at Malta on January 16.

January 18.   *Ohio* and *Missouri* leave Athens bound for Salonica.

January 19.   *Illinois, Kearsarge,* and *Wisconsin* depart Malta for Algiers, arriving at the Algerian port on the 24th. They are joined three days later by *Kentucky*.

January 20.   *Connecticut* departs Naples to rejoin the rest of First Division at Villefranche.

January 31.	First Battleship Division arrives at Gibraltar.
February 1.	The balance of the Great White Fleet arrives at The Rock.
February 5.	Captain Edward F. Qualtrough is relieved of command of *Georgia*, accused of drunkenness. New skipper is Lieutenant-Commander George F. Kline.
February 6.	The Great White Fleet departs Gibraltar and heads for Hampton Roads.
February 14.	Rear Admiral Conway H. Arnold leaves Hampton Roads to meet Sperry's globetrotters. Arnold flies his flag aboard *Maine*, steaming with battleships *New Hampshire*, *Mississippi*, and *Idaho*, with two armored and three scout cruisers.
February 17.	Arnold's escort makes the link up with Sperry's task force.
February 22.	The Great White Fleet and escort force arrive at Hampton Roads on George Washington's birthday. President Roosevelt reviews the fleet. Cruise declared officially over. It takes fourteen months and six days to complete for a steam of 46,729 miles.

TABLE FOUR
BATTLESHIP FACTS & TIDBITS

- The sixteen battleships sent round the world by President Theodore Roosevelt on December 16, 1907, have been known ever since as the Great White Fleet. In reality, American warships had been painted white since the 1880s. The color made American ships very distinctive and easily identifiable. It also made American ships lovely targets, as was realized during the round-the-world cruise. Upon the fleet's return, American warships were painted gray.

- Throughout the narrative American battleships were frequently referred to by their alphanumeric designations. For example, USS *Connecticut* was BB-18, USS *Vermont* was BB-20, USS *Kearsarge* was BB-05, and so on. On July 20, 1920, the U.S. Navy instituted the alphanumeric designation "BB" for each and every battleship. Ships authorized prior to July 20 were simply back numbered. Ships after July 20 simply carried forward the "BB" designation until the last battleship had been authorized.

- Just what is a battleship? A battleship is a heavy duty man-of-war—a floating steel fortress bulging with thick armor and bristling with massive guns, able to send tons of explosives out to a distance beyond where the eye can see. In the nineteenth century, these warships were known as the "Main Line of Battle Ship," which was eventually abbreviated to battleship. The evolution of the American battleship went through four stages: The second-class or prototype battleship, the pre-dreadnought, the dreadnought, and lastly the fast battleship. The two examples of the second-class battleship were the ill-fated *Maine* (not to be confused with the later pre-dreadnought BB-10) and *Texas*. Despite the ten-inch guns carried on the former and the twelve-inch rifles mounted on the latter, these vessels displaced under 6,700 tons and were really armored cruisers. The same can be said of the later German pocket battleships *Graf Spee, Admiral Scheer,* and *Lutzow.* They boasted a main armament of six eleven-inch rifles. But the ships were equivalent in size to heavy cruisers and were later reclassified as such by the Germans.

The next step in the evolution of the American battleship was the pre-dreadnought. USS *Indiana* (BB-01) was the first real battleship built by the United States. She displaced over 10,000 tons and carried a mixed armament of thirteen-inch, eight-inch, and six-inch guns. Despite increases in size and speed, the following twenty-four battleships were of this type.

The advent of HMS *Dreadnought* revolutionized battleship design. Carrying a main armament of ten twelve-inch guns and with a top speed of twenty-one knots, *Dreadnought* (which means "Fear Nothing but God") rendered every other battleship in the world obsolete. The United States was already building two comparable ships with USS *South Carolina* (BB-26) and USS *Michigan*

(BB-27). Each mounted eight twelve-inch rifles but were rather slow at 18.5 knots. Twenty more dreadnought battleships followed. Each succeeding class was an improvement over the last in terms of size and fire power. This type of American battleship culminated with the USS *Colorado* (BB-45), USS *Maryland,* (BB-46) and USS *West Virginia* (BB-48). Each mounted eight sixteen-inch guns and weighed more than 33,000 tons.

The final stage in the evolution of American battleship design was the fast battleship. Beginning with USS *North Carolina* (BB-55) and ending with USS *Wisconsin* (BB-64), these ten battlewagons mounted nine sixteen-inch rifles and displaced 41,000 to 58,000 tons at full load. These leviathans were speedy enough to keep up with the fast carrier task forces; and, with their bristling array of firepower, they proved invaluable in protecting the precious carriers from air attack. And while battleship-to-battleship engagements were rare in World War II, their powerful main armament was essential in the support of soldiers and marines during the many amphibious operations in the Atlantic and Pacific theaters of war.

- Battleships boasted the largest guns ever mounted on warships. These were major-caliber weapons capable of firing heavy projectiles out to many thousands of yards. The caliber of the gun was determined by the inside diameter of the barrel. The barrels were rifled with what were known as lands and grooves. The raised part of the rifling were the lands, while the depressions in between were the grooves. The diameter of the barrel is determined from the top of the lands across the widest point of the tube. The barrel's length is determined by multiplying its diameter. For example, flagship of the Great White Fleet, USS *Connecticut* (BB-18), mounted a twelve-inch 45 caliber gun. The caliber in length is figured by multiplying the diameter, which is twelve inches, by the caliber, which is 45. Barrel length then is 540 inches. This leads to an interesting comparison. The *Connecticut* class was the epitome of American pre-dreadnought design. Each of their twelve-inch guns threw an 870-pound projectile out to an effective range of fifteen thousand yards at a velocity of 2,850 feet-per-second. In stark contrast was the *Iowa*. The fast battleships of the *Iowa* class stand as the epitome of American battleship design. Each of their sixteen-inch rifles could throw a 2,700-pound projectile out to an effective range of forty-one thousand yards at a velocity of 2,800 feet per second. Such was the evolution in technology that increased the battleship's ability to project greater amounts of power over vaster distances.

- Throughout the narrative, there are numerous references to the etiquette of gun salutes. For the reader who is unfamiliar with this form of military courtesy, there are varying numbers of gun salutes depending on the stature of the person saluted. For instance, the President of the United States (including ex-presidents) was accorded a twenty-one-gun salute, as were foreign heads of state. The vice-president, state governors, ambassadors, high commissioners, secretary of defense, secretaries of any of the services, and foreign prime ministers received a nineteen-gun salute. Generals and admirals of the highest ranking got a seventeen-gun salute. Lieutenant-generals and vice admirals got fifteen-gun salutes, while major-generals and rear admirals were accorded thirteen-gun salutes, and so on down the line. It should be noticed that all gun salutes are odd numbers. Why this is so has never been fully explained. But gun salutes go back many centuries. Britain, however, standardized the twenty-one-gun salute in 1730 for certain dates of significance. Later it was included to salute the royal family. In 1818, the U.S. Navy made it mandatory that when the president visited a ship, he was to be accorded a twenty-one-gun salute. On August 17, 1875, the United States accepted the British proposal for recognizing the twenty-one-gun salute as an international form of accepted military etiquette.

With the army and marine corps, the firing of a twenty-one-gun salute with artillery pieces for the President of the United States or visiting head of state was consistent with navy practices. However, "Final Honors" for veterans are not gun salutes. This is because to a soldier or marine, a rifle is not a gun. When a veteran is laid to rest, seven riflemen, upon command, fire three volleys for a total of twenty-one shots. While undoubtedly a salute of the utmost respect, it is nonetheless considered "three volleys."

- All sixteen pre-dreadnoughts of the Great White Fleet were battleships, not battle cruisers. The battle cruiser was the brainchild of the redoubtable Jackie Fisher of England. Jackie Fisher was the power behind the revolutionary HMS *Dreadnought*. When this man-of-war appeared on the scene, it rendered every other battleship in the world obsolete. At the time of her launch, *Dreadnought* was a superior blend of armor, speed, and hitting power. The battle cruiser was different. It rivaled the battleship in size and firepower, but had noticeably greater speed. The battle cruiser was designed as an oversized scout for the main battle fleet. With its dreadnought-like firepower, it could dispatch any normal-sized cruiser that might be encountered. At the Falkland Islands on December 8, 1914, British Admiral Doveton Sturdee employed the battle cruisers *Invincible* and *Inflexible* to defeat German Admiral Graf von Spee's force of light and armored cruisers. Spee's heaviest ships were the armored cruisers *Scharnhorst* and *Gneisenau*, which were armed with 8.2-inch guns versus the twelve-inch rifles mounted on Sturdee's battle cruisers. The British commander's greater weight of firepower enabled him to decisively defeat his German opponent. However, at Jutland in 1916, it was a different story, for this clash of heavyweights exposed the battle cruiser's dangerous flaw: A lack of armor. The vessel's superior speed came at the expense of protection. In the slugfest off the Skagerrak, the eleven- and twelve-inch guns of the German battle fleet blew up three of the lightly armored British battle cruisers. Germany also lost a battle cruiser. Only one battleship was sunk on either side, the German *Pommern*, an outdated predreadnought. Heavy armor had won out over greater speed.

Twenty-five years later, history repeated itself with the demise of HMS *Hood*. This famous ship went up against the *Bismarck* and was promptly dispatched with calamitous results that saw only three of her crew of 1,519 survive. Thin deck armor once again proved ineffective against the plunging fire of massive guns. By World War II, battleships like the *Bismarck, King George V, Iowa,* and *Yamato* had rendered the battle cruiser obsolete, for these were capital ships of battle cruiser speed and battleship protection.

The United States dabbled with the battle cruiser during World War II in the form of two warships known as the *Alaska* and *Guam.* These large cruisers mounted nine twelve-inch guns and could cut through the water at thirty-three knots. When compared to the fast battleships coming out of American yards, these large cruisers were undergunned and underarmored. The rest of the class was canceled. They would have been named as follows: *Hawaii, Philippines, Puerto Rico,* and *Samoa.* Unlike battleships, which were named for states, large cruisers were named for U.S. territories.

BIBLIOGRAPHY

BOOKS

Albertson, Mark. *USS Connecticut: Constitution State Battleship*. Tate Publishing: Mustang, Oklahoma, 2007.

Bennett, Geoffrey. *Naval Battles of the First World War*. B.T. Botsford Ltd.: London, 1968.

Bywater, Hector C., *Sea Power in the Pacific: A Study of the American-Japanese Naval Problem*. Houghton, Mifflin Co.: Boston, 1921.

Carr, William. *A History of Germany, 1815–1945*. St. Martin's Press: New York, 1969.

Carter, Samuel III. *The Incredible Great White Fleet*. Collier's: New York, 1971.

Craven, Avery. *Reconstruction: The Ending of the Civil War*. Holt, Rinehart and Winston: New York, 1969.

Foote, Shelby. *The Civil War, A Narrative: From Fort Sumter to Perryville*. Random House: New York, 1958.

Friedman, Norman. *U.S. Battleships, An Illustrative Design History*. Naval Institute Press: Annapolis, 1985.

Hale, Oron J. *The Great Illusion, 1900–1914.* Harper & Row: New York, 1971.

Hill, Richard. *War at Sea in the Ironclad Age.* Cassell & Co.: Wellington House, London, 2000.

Hough, Richard. *The Fleet That Had to Die.* Ballantine Books, New York, 1958.

Jackson, Robert. *The World's Great Battleships.* Brown Books Ltd.: London, 2000.

Kennedy, Paul. *Pacific Onslaught: 7th Dec. 1941/Feb. 1943.* Ballantine Books: New York, 1972.

Konstam, Angus. *Duel of the Ironclads: USS Monitor & CSS Virginia at Hampton Roads, 1862.* Osprey Publishing: Oxford, 2003.

Linthicum, Richard. *War Between Japan and Russia.* W.R. Vansant: Chicago, 1905.

Massie, Robert K. *Dreadnought: Britain and Germany and the Coming of the Great War.* Random House: New York, 1991.

Newhart, Max R. *American Battleships: A Pictorial History of BB-1 to BB-71.* Pictorial Histories Publishing Co.: Missoula, 1995.

Padfield, Peter. *Battleship.* Birlinn Limited: Edinburgh, 2000.

Pringle, Henry F. *Theodore Roosevelt: A Biography.* Harcourt, Brace and Co.: New York, 1931.

Reckner, James R. *Teddy Roosevelt's Great White Fleet.* Naval Institute Press: Annapolis, 1988.

Steam, Steel and Shellfire: The Steam Warship, 1815–1905: Conway's History of the Ship. Conway Maritime Press: 1992.

Stevens, William Oliver and Westcott, Allen. *A History of Sea Power.* Doubleday Doran & Co., Inc.: Garden City, 1937.

Storry, Richard. *A History of Modern Japan.* Penguin Books: Middlesex, 1960.

The Illustrated Encyclopedia of 20th Century Weapons and Warfare, Vol. 1, *Ai/AMX,* Vol. 8, *Dr 1/F 50,* Vol. 13, *Holt/Inva, Vol. 15, Karl/Kriv.* Columbia House: New York, 1967.

The Japanese War Machine, ed. By S.L.A. Mayer, Bison Books, London, 1976.

Tuchman, Barbara. *The Zimmerman Telegram.* Macmillan Publishing Co.: New York, 1958.

Warner, Denis and Peggy. *The Tide at Sunrise: A History of the Russo-Japanese War, 1904–1905.* Charter Books: New York, 1974.

Welty, Paul Thomas. *The Asians: Their Heritage and Their Destiny.* J.P. Lippincott, Co.: Philadelphia, 1962.

Wimmel, Kenneth. *Theodore Roosevelt and the Great White Fleet.* Brassey's: Virginia, 1998.

MISCELLANEOUS SOURCES

Albertson, Mark. "When Connecticut led the Great White Fleet." *Connecticut Post,* October 10, 2004.

"Fightin' Bob Evans," *The Connector.* Connecticut States Public Library Newsletter, Vol. 4, No. 4, November 2002.

"Great Battles of the Civil War," by the editors of Life, Time Inc. New York, 1961.

Milton, Keith. "Duel at Hampton Roads." *Military Heritage,* December 2001.

Navy Department, Office of the Chief of Naval Operations, Division of Naval History, (OP 09B9) Ships' Histories Section, *History of Ships Named Connecticut.*

Strait, Raymond. "The Cage Mast Fleet." *Battleships at War! Sea Classics Magazine* Special, Fall 1984.

End of the World

[1] *History of Ships Named Connecticut.* Navy Department, Office of the Chief of Naval Operations, Division of Naval History (OP O9B9). Ships' Histories Section. pg. 8

[2] Reckner, James. *Teddy Roosevelt's Great White Fleet.* Annapolis: Naval Institute Press, 1988. pg. 44

Down Under

[1] Albertson, Mark. *USS Connecticut: Constitution State Battleship.* Mustang, Tate Publishing: 2007. pg. 50

There's No Place Like Home

[1] *History of Ships Named Connecticut.* Navy Department, Office of the Chief of Naval Operations, Division of Naval History (OP 09B9). Ships' Histories Section. pg. 14

Table One: Disposition of the Great White Fleet

[1] U.S. Navy Department. *Information Relative to the Voyage of the United States Atlantic Fleet Around the World, December 16, 1907 to February 22, 1909.* Washington, D.C.: Government Printing Office, 1910.

Table Three: Chronology of the Great White Fleet

[1] Based on a condensed log of the cruise. www.mars.ark.com/~camorris/gwfleet/gwfleet1.htm. Hampton Roads to San Francisco. Morris, Cheryl.